AWKWARDLY AWESOME
ENDORSEMENTS

"A book is written once every decade that changes lives more than any other book... Jason Freeman's book *Awkwardly Awesome* is that book of this decade and beyond. Jason literally took what most would consider his greatest liabilities, a speech impediment and coordination problem and turned them on their heads to become his greatest assets!

Jason tamed his coordination awkwardness with yoga and accentuated his speech impediment by becoming a rock-solid motivational speaker... and may I add, one of my favorites! Get ready to ignite your life in a positive direction as your read this amazing book!"

~ DENIS NURMELA
TheYESman.org

"With a winning combination of practical inspiration and heart-felt autobiography, Jason reminds us not only of the importance but the necessity of bravely going for our dreams."

~ FRANK SHANKWITZ
Creator and a Founder of the Make-A-Wish Foundation and
Motivational Speaker, wishman1.com

"Jason enlightens us with the transformation process that most of us experience in stunning silence. I love this story. I love that we all have our Awkward Awesomeness and I love that after reading this book, many, many will discover, celebrate and share theirs."

~ DAVID M. CORBIN
Author of *Preventing BrandSlaughter*, and *Illuminate*
Mentor to Mentors

"I've been honored to have Jason speak at several of my Evolving Out Loud events—his open heart and sense of humor is a gift to us all."

~ KYLE CEASE
Author of *I Hope I Screw This Up: How Falling In Love with Your Fears Can Change the World*

"Courageous, humble, inspiring--and perfectly imperfect. Jason's authenticity is contagious, and can help you grow your own seed of greatness."

~ TAL BEN-SHAHAR
Best-selling author of *Choose the Life You Want*

"I first saw Jason speak on Kyle Cease's Evolving Out Loud stage 2 years ago in Venice, California and it stopped me in my tracks. I burst into tears right in the front row! His story broke my heart wide open. I gained a deep respect for his brilliance and bravery. His storytelling showed me that I too, was holding myself back because of "a war within". Each of us have personal battles that are largely fought or lost alone. Jason's talk illuminated that for me. I was inspired to work with him in his Talk Swap process. We've been working together weekly ever since and it's no lie to admit that our Skype sessions have freed me to reach dreams and go deep to places I had not imagined possible. Here is his story. I highly recommend his first book and, if you need a breakthrough from a limited mindset or a closed up heart, Jason is the coach for you.

~ TRACI ROBINSON
Storyteller, performer, coach and multi-million dollar real estate broker in the Hamptons.

"*Awkwardly Awesome* is chock full of the imperfect and the wonderful."

~ BEN GAY III
The Closers, BFG3.com

"Jason Freeman is a man that not only has an authentic and true heart and the compassion of 1000 men, but also the courage of a warrior!

Joining Jason on his perfect journey of imperfection will be one of the greatest gifts you can give yourself.

To say you'll be inspired is a huge understatement. You'll be transformed!"

~MIKE KEMSKI
#1 Bestselling author *Change Your Energy, Change Your Life!*,
MikeKemski.com

"With a refreshing mix of humble autobiography and practical insight, Jason brings joy to the often painfully serious business of self-improvement.

Jason is Smart, Daring and Different. That makes him the very special person he is!"

~ RON KLEIN
The Grandfather of Possibilities, Inventor of the Magnetic Strip on the credit card, validity checking system and more.

"Brilliant" does not just describe Jason's unique perspective (it is) …. Brilliant is the intensity of the light with which Jason Freeman illuminates the darkness of self-doubt that engulfs each of us from time to time. If you find yourself dealing with the fear of being less than perfect - and who doesn't? - this book is for you. Jason's words have helped me experience everyone - including myself - with more compassion. *Awkwardly Awesome* is an 'awesomely' inspiring guidebook to a more joy-filled life in this magnificently perfect imperfect world!"

~ JEFF SALZ, PH.D., CPAE
Author of *The Way of Adventure*

"It's every man and woman's desire to strive to go from imperfect to perfect in their lives, only to gain the realization that imperfect is indeed perfect! Jason Freeman instills this in you, as the reader, and takes you through the journey from shoe strings to all-important acorn principles! Allow Jason to "WOW" you as he did me. This is why he has an open invitation for life to speak on any of my Habitude Warrior Conference stages which typically boasts a 2 year waiting list. Way to go Jason! Keep changing lives one day at a time."

~ ERIK "MR. AWESOME" SWANSON
Speaker, coach, CEO Habitude Warrior Int.
www.HabitudeWarrior.com

"When I met Jason Freeman, before he became the speaker, yoga instructor, writer and coach he is today, he barely spoke a word. Jason was worried about being understood (or misunderstood), about saying something wrong, about how he stood and walked, and it showed. As we became friends, I discovered his huge heart and passionate commitment to connect, love and serve others even if it was uncomfortable for him. Jason began posting on Facebook every day, even those days when he didn't think he had anything to say. First text, then photographs, then video, then speaking on podcasts, radio shows, to groups and on stages and now this timely and wonderful book, Awkwardly Awesome. Jason leads by example, teaching that we are the only ones who can get in our own way of really living full out. It's our imperfections that make us human, loved and loving. His courage in going first makes it possible for the rest of us to believe in him and ourselves. Thank you for being my friend and one of the most inspiring human beings I have ever known!"

~ ALISON BW PENA
International speaker and Life-to-Legacy consultant
BadWidow.com, AffluenceCode.com

More praise about Awkwardly Awesome
and Jason Freeman at the end of this book.

AWKWARDLY AWESOME

EMBRACING MY IMPERFECT BEST

by

jason w. freeman

Imperfect Best Book Series

HEROIC PRODUCTIONS YES!

Published by
Heroic Yes! Productions LLC
www.HeroicYesProductions.com

Cover design by Chris Taylor - www.creative-beard.com
Cover illustration by Lamont Hunt - www.DakotaKidCreations.com
Book design by Chris Taylor - www.creative-beard.com

Cover & Author photographs © 2017 Chris Taylor
Additional cover photographs by Getty Images

Awkwardly Awesome: Embracing My Imperfect Best
By Jason W. Freeman, B.A., M.F.A.
Edited by Tonie Harrington - watb2017@gmail.com

ISBN 978-0-9987344-0-8
eBook ISBN 978-0-9987344-1-5

SEL021000 SELF-HELP / Motivational & Inspirational
SEL016000 SELF-HELP / Personal Growth / Happiness
SEL023000 SELF-HELP / Personal Growth / Self-Esteem

First Edition: Published April 2017

www.JasonWFreeman.com
www.HeroicYesProductions.com
Facebook/MrJasonWFreeman

DEDICATION

To our ancestors who did their imperfect best
to create this abundant world we live in today.

May we do our imperfect best
to steward their gift and pass it on
to our grandchildren's great-grandchildren.

CONTENTS

ACKNOWLEDGEMENTS

My parents who've cherished me as a gift since the day I was born. My Mom also did one of the final edits on the book. Thanks Mom!

All my English teachers from grade school through grad school. I dearly love writing. Thanks for nurturing this love.

Rachel Labarre: I came to Rachel, one of my beloved yoga teachers and said, "I want to write a book. I have a thousand page tangle of random ideas and twice that many in my head." She said, "Take a deep breath," and proceeded to give me writing assignments that would become the initial rough draft of my book. Thanks Rachel for getting me past the point of overwhelm to the point of enjoying the process.

Tonie Harrington: I posted on Facebook that I was writing a book. She sent me a Facebook message that she would love to edit it. Little did she know that editing it would turn into a huge project. This book is so many times better than it might have been because I answered her message with a YES! Thanks from the bottom of my heart Tonie. You are brilliant!

Mark Lamaster: I hadn't seen Mark since college. He found me on Facebook and said, "I've written a book. I have practical knowledge that could help you." Mark did not disappoint. He gave that practical knowledge very generously.

Chris Taylor: The guru of all things technical in my business from my sizzle reel, to my website, to the layout of this book, its cover and even the author photograph. Everybody needs a few gurus. Chris is definitely one of mine.

Lamont Hunt: Lamont is a dear friend who has become an artistic genius. Chris and I asked him to illustrate some clothing on me . . . track clothing! For the cover! Not only did he exceed our expectations, he somehow made me look great in running gear!

It's taken me a lifetime filled with loving family and friendships to have the courage to write this book. I would love to thank each beloved person individually, but that would be a book in and of itself. So I will simply take this occasion to say Thank You!

FORWARD

This book exists because a fresh path to living has become available to me. I had heard tell of its existence, but didn't believe it was accessible to people like me. For most of my life, I chose the path of being ashamed of, and trying to cover up what I thought was most imperfect about me. I possess both extremely visible and not-so-noticeable imperfections that seem all but invisible to the outside world.

However, unlike many people, my noticeable imperfections are defined as a disability. When I was born, my umbilical cord got kinked like a garden hose, resulting in a loss of oxygen that left me with a pronounced speech impediment and coordination differences. Cerebral palsy is the general term used to describe the disorders caused by that loss of oxygen.

For example, if we were sitting in a cafe talking right now, you would notice that I talk slower than 99% of people and that sometimes it sounds like I'm hammered. But I'm neither slow nor drunk. It's just my normal everyday speech pattern. As for my lack of coordination, during a track meet in seventh grade, I actually threw a shot put backwards. True story!

As a result of those imperfections, I fought myself for years. **Do you know what it's like to be at war with yourself?** I declared war on my imperfections and tried to battle my way beyond them. I spent twenty-five years on the warpath with myself. I wish I could tell you that, as I traveled further along this path, I started to win more and more battles. But the truth is that the warpath consumed me. I hustled for perfection, but all I gained was a high level of stress and self-loathing that threw me into frequent periods of sadness and frustration. This wasn't the life that I knew in my heart I was capable of living and wanted to live in my heart. I wanted more, but didn't know where to find it.

I've written this book because I've finally found a fresh path—a path that takes great courage, because the first step requires that we acknowledge what we perceive as wrong with ourselves. This can be a frightening path, and many people never walk down it for any number of reasons.

When an individual acknowledges their perceived imperfections, they arrive at a fork in the road. One branch of that fork continues down the path of reliving the same story and expressing the same pain over and over and over again.

The second branch is a journey into the unknown. It involves asking ourselves questions about what those imperfections could possibly mean besides the stories we've kept reciting to ourselves over the years. **That second branch also provides different options to meet our perceived imperfections head on and possibly move forward rather than stagnating.**

This is **a frightening path, because it** changes who we think we are and how we understand and interact with the world. It **changes our core assumptions about our self- worth.**

A basic part of human nature is to fight change, because change will likely bring all manner of emotions to the surface, emotions we have been afraid to experience. It's tempting, therefore, to turn back to the same actions, feelings, and outcomes—the same denial, the same false smiles of contentment, and the familiar pretense that everything is all right, even though deep down we know that everything is not all right.

It can be absolutely agonizing to step beyond what we know. We come up with endless excuses as to why this first step won't work, is a waste of time, is dangerous and will end in failure. The relieving news is that it only takes a brief trek down this courageous path to get started. That first step brings us further along than we've ever been before. **The process of turning our limitations into our jet fuel is the process of taking that first step followed by another.**

Be aware that there may not always be that big "A-Ha!" moment that suddenly turns your imperfections into a life of bliss. I've found it's more of a gradual process of stepping up to the bright mountaintop and beholding the view. Occasionally we may slip into a dark valley where we flounder in search of the light. It's a challenging journey, but I've learned that the **rewarding epiphanies come from the daily effort to find the light.**

There's no way I could have aligned with my best life until I aligned with the perfection of my speech impediment and lack of coordination. They are perfect because they express the wholeness of who I am. This discovery simply wasn't available to me when I was on the warpath against myself.

In this book, I talk about my trek down that warpath and how my war almost consumed me; however, through many difficult twists and turns I discovered a fresh path.

It's utterly important to understand that the more

fully we learn to express ourselves as we really are, the more we can enhance our quality of life and the quality of life of those around us.

I hope my journey and the things I've accomplished so far will serve as encouragement for you as you embark on your journey to turn your limitations into jet fuel. Most of all, I want to impart to you that **this journey is within your capabilities. The human capacity to grow and adapt is unlimited. You deserve to be happy and live out your dreams.**

The following pages contain autobiographical reminiscences, and a few questions sprinkled in for self-introspection and inspiration. I know I have turned my imperfections into jet fuel, and I believe I can help you do the same. Hopefully, someday soon I will write a book filled with stories of clients who have successfully found their way from their personal warpath to a fresh path using my methods.

I've come to believe that **doing our "imperfect best" is one of the most powerful things we can do for ourselves and the world.** I use the phrase "imperfect best" to describe a liberating attitude towards life. Doing **our imperfect best means accepting that there will often be mistakes, flaws, and rough edges. These mistakes, flaws, and rough edges add to the beauty of who we are and provide us with the power to connect with others.**

I am inviting you to travel this path of self-acceptance and enhanced self-worth with me. It's a difficult, but wonderful journey, and I know that it works. I believe you, too, will find your personal path of self-acceptance and self-worth.

IMPERFECT BEST REFLECTIONS

A Section Just For You

What has been a change that you have made in your life that has felt really good?

What has been the significance of this change for you?

What's the importance of making peace with ourselves?

INTRODUCTION

A Letter To My Seven-Year-Old Self

Hey Kiddo,

You are so cute! You love to run around with your shoestrings untied and imagine the world just the way you want it. You love making plans for what you will be when you grow up, and you love changing those plans every other day. You do this because you can. You do this because life delights you and there's just so much to do. It seems so easy to succeed in life.

You love your Mom. You love your Papa. You declare yourself the President of the Land on which you and your Mom and Papa live. Mom gets out poster board and writes "The Rules of the Land" as you dictate. You are always thinking about making the world a better place Little Man, and it's good to see that you are starting close to home.

As Mom and Dad tuck you in, they tell you, "I love you. Sleep tight." They also frequently say, "You are the best." Yes, you are the answer to their prayers. They see you so clearly as the miracle you are.

As of yet, you haven't begun your long and brutal campaign of focusing on what your body can't do. Your voice is still perfect to you. You fit into your body like a comfortable pair of tennis shoes, just right for your exploration of your world. Aglow with happiness, you have no sense that you could ever feel any differently about yourself.

You look at grown-ups in awe, but at the same time wonder why they aren't as free and as fun as kids are. When you are grown up, you are determined to be different.

But "grown-up" will come all too quickly for you. Too soon your voice will begin to sound to you like nails on a chalkboard. Too soon, gym class will become less and less fun as you begin to keep score and compare yourself to the other kids. Too soon, you will find that, at least in your mind, you are constantly losing. And you're gonna hate to lose.

Practice, Kiddo! Remember to practice and

practice. Remember that by practicing over and over again you already have learned to walk and talk.

You are going to become very tempted to substitute the words, "I can't," and "It's so unfair," for your winning attitude of "I'll practice until I get it."

Sure, some people will seem to pick up things twice as fast as you. They are running their race. You are running yours, simple as that. But you are going to be sorely tempted to make things infinitely more complex for yourself. You are going to try to diminish other people's accomplishments so you feel better. You are going to try to convince yourself that if something requires too much practice, it's probably not that much fun to achieve anyway.

You are going to try to talk yourself out of striving for your dreams. However, Kiddo, an attempt to make your life easier by not going for your dreams actually works in reverse. Life becomes infinitely more complex when you're bored, because you have systematically removed challenging activities from your life. To put it simply, when you are bored you will start to worry, obsess, stress out, create drama, engage in vicious hypochondria, and generally feel miserable in your awkwardness. When you're bored, you will make the sound of your voice and your unique coordination into a major, epic disability. When you are bored, you will become morbidly afraid of one day dying.

Let me give you the Cliff Notes version on this one: If you are bored and not challenging yourself by practicing the things you truly want to do, you are going to feel like you are withering and dying.

Living fully is about breathing deeply, showing up, laughing, and playing. So, find more and more and more things in life that fascinate you and that you love. Then practice them everyday with all your heart.

If you give something a try and it's still making you miserable after you've given it a fair shake, by all means stop doing it and move on to something else. There are plenty of other options. There is absolutely no reason to make long-term plans to do something that only makes you feel miserable.

For example, fear of there not being enough money can become a tough addiction. So, to make money you will be tempted to do things that you feel like crud doing. There are countless "another day, another dollar" jobs out there. Fear could keep you in a job like this for twenty-five or thirty years. Remember that if you cloud that precious smile of yours by doing work that you despise, there simply won't be enough time to do the things you love.

When you love the work you do you are much more likely to practice and practice until you develop a talent for it. So search constantly until you find work to which you can give your heart. Let the world pay you abundantly for your talent and your heart. Understand, though, that it may take quite a while to get paid "abundantly" for your talent and your heart. But, it is truly worth the journey. The money you make from doing what you love will feel infinitely more valuable than money you would make from doing things that weigh you down with fear. Let your career be your teacher, guiding you to become the person you most want to be.

Get rich quick schemes won't teach you this, so don't waste energy pining after them and chasing them. But, if a million dollars falls into your lap without much effort, thank your lucky stars and take it.

Use all money that comes into your life to enhance your experience. Be generous. Don't get lazy or too comfortable. Laziness creates boredom. If you need a refresher on what boredom does, please re-read the above.

Here's an important word to never forget— TRUST! Kiddo, notice how naturally you trust yourself right now. At your age you don't even think twice about it. You go with your ideas, instincts and intuition. Soon, however, you will start convincing yourself that others know better than you. You will convince yourself that you ought to defer to others because you have a speech impediment and coordination problems. You will quiet yourself because you feel your voice is less important than other voices. This tactic may make sense in your pre-teenage brain as a way to cope.

But, Little Brilliant One, realize that quieting the best in you won't help you grow into the person you want to be, and definitely won't help the world evolve into what it wants to be.

In about thirty years you might discover this Marianne Williamson quote, but I'm going to give it to you a bit earlier and hope you understand:

> "Our deepest fear is not that we are inadequate. Our deepest fear is that we are powerful beyond measure. It is our light, not our darkness that most frightens us. We ask ourselves, 'Who am I to be brilliant, gorgeous, talented, fabulous?' Actually, who are you not to be? You are a child of God. Your playing small does not serve the world. There is nothing enlightened about shrinking so that other

people won't feel insecure around you. We are all meant to shine, as children do. We were born to make manifest the glory of God that is within us. It's not just in some of us; it's in everyone. And as we let our own light shine, we unconsciously give other people permission to do the same. As we are liberated from our own fear, our presence automatically liberates others."

MARIANNE WILLIAMSON
A Return to Love: Reflections on the Principles of a Course in Miracles, Harper Collins, 1992. Pg. 190-191)

Yes, Jason Freeman, even as a boy you are a Free Man. But as you quiet yourself out of fear that what you really think and feel is not good enough to be said, your freedom will be diminished and the world will be less free because of your silence. So speak up and speak proud when you convey the truth within you.

At the same time, always be conscious that you are a healer. Use your words for healing. Always speak your truth as kindly as possible. (Note: You might develop a habit of being sarcastic and coarse at certain points in your life. Cut them both out. Neither represents who you truly are.)

Life becomes so much easier when you speak your truth and follow your intuition.

While we are on this subject you might try on many masks in life. As soon as you notice that you are putting one on, it's time to take it off. Remember, wearing a mask quickly becomes hot and claustrophobic. Furthermore, masks don't fool people who are comfortable in their own skin for long. They spot trickery and move away.

Kiddo, you want to attract people to you who are comfortable in their own skin. They can help you heal and call you on the things you are trying to hide.

(Note: Speaking of comfortable in your own skin, when you read this, the word "yoga" will look to you like a misspelling of the word yogurt. After all, right now you live in South Dakota in the 80's. Nevertheless, find out what this word means as soon as you possibly can. Find books on it, and take a class at the soonest opportunity. Otherwise you might wait till you're thirty-two to stumble into a yoga class. You are meant to move. But fear of looking awkward as you move will most likely keep you from playing contact sports. Don't sweat it. Chronic stress and worry find safe harbor in a body that doesn't move. The stagnant waters become a murky breeding ground for the multitude of sea monsters the mind can create. Try to find yoga. Learn to breathe. Consistently stretch your body in all ways possible.)

Seven-year-old Jason Freeman, "organization" isn't your middle name. William is. Your Mom will get a wee bit frustrated with you for losing the red uniform sweater in that adorable picture of you, and many more like it. Your room is often a mess. This all seems fun now, but I tell you, your life will expand as you find ways to organize yourself and do so on a consistent basis. A human drives more cars and lives in more houses than an ant because a human has organized his or her world much more intricately than an ant has.

You can apply the same idea to your own life. You can either vigorously resist organization, which you are doing quite an impressive job at so far I must say, or you can figure out how to organize your life and then watch as you create the things you want to create and feel far more relaxed doing it.

The wisdom I'm imparting to you now is based on years of personal experience, but it might not be meant for you yet. Maybe you are meant to go down all the roads I'm trying to dissuade you from traveling. Maybe all those roads have made me into a man capable of writing this letter to you now. Just remember, my Brilliant Young Self, that life is such a mystery. Delight in it. Accept its challenges.

I look forward to seeing you in 34 years.

IMPERFECT
BEST
REFLECTIONS

A Section Just For You

What are the top three nuggets of wisdom you would offer your seven-year-old self?

What's the funniest thing you would tell your seven-year-old self?

What's the thing you would tell your seven-year-old self that most surprises you?

Chapter 1
PERFECTLY IMPERFECT

I've been trying to write the perfect book since high school. The results are in a large Rubbermaid tub in my closet. I don't know what all is in there, but I do know that the tub makes a great stepping stool when I want to organize my socks on the top shelf of my closet.

This book isn't going to be perfect. Even after forty-one years on this earth, that's almost enough to drive me crazy and throw me back into The-Planning-To-Write-The-Perfect-Book-Phase, the endless brainstorming, the boundless free writing that creates a library of notebooks. Part of my life's purpose is to write lots of books. Yet, at the moment, I use the majority of my writing as a stepping stool. Yes! That joke's definitely on me.

Are there any green Rubbermaid tubs full of brilliance stashed away in your life?

My plan for this "perfectly imperfect" book is to create a conversational autobiography. Hopefully, it will become **a two-way conversation, so that when I ask questions** like whether you have a Rubbermaid tub hidden somewhere in your life, **you'll take a moment to think about it and respond, just as though we were conversing in a coffee shop.**

As you read this, you can't hear my unique "Jason-from-Sioux-Falls-South-Dakota-Midwestern-accent," because I don't have one. Rather my unique accent stems from a speech impediment. I'm also able to hide my lack of coordination from you that causes me to move somewhat awkwardly. These are the advantages of writing a book instead of meeting you in person. I can hide those imperfections.

Today, however, I'm not writing to hide myself from you. **I'm writing because our individual uniquenesses have the power to draw us into community, the power to bring us out of hiding and into the fullness of what our lives can be.**

If I didn't have a speech impediment and coordination differences, would I be so inspired to connect with large numbers of people through public speaking? I don't know. Part of me is highly introverted and loves to go on long walks by myself for hours on end. That part of me has about as much interest in speaking to large groups as I have in going to the dentist every week.

But there's another part of me that's definitely inspired to communicate with as many people as I can with love and clarity. If everything had been just fine and dandy with my speech and coordination would this inspiration still be there? Who knows?

For much of my life I despised my speech impediment and coordination differences. You'll note I use the past tense—despised. Now I'm growing to deeply love my speech impediment and lack of coordination. Why? My attitude didn't change because my body magically became "normal." **I learned to love myself because I finally noticed that my body was magic and perfect just** as is. I REPEAT—I learned to love myself because I finally noticed that my body was magic and perfect just as is.

"As is" is always changing anyway. How we view our lives or ourselves is never fixed. There's nothing huge you need to do at any moment other than to take a few deep breaths and be open to viewing yourself in new ways. This all takes time, but why not?

The fear and desire to be perfect wasn't in me as a little kid, as near as I can remember. I was so lucky. I was born to two loving parents who believed in me and gave me a very strong foundation.

I'm seven years old and it's the height of July. Outside is My Territory. This territory seems unbelievably vast because we live in the country on a large piece of land. There are giant oaks as ominous as mean giants, dandelions as yellow as the sun, butterflies as unexplainable as magic. I dash around in flip flops with a knotted bunch of shoe strings in my hands all the while living out every dream a seven year old boy can imagine in his head.

This habit that seemed utterly normal to me at the time seems mighty peculiar as I look back on it. **When was the time in your life when you dreamed the biggest?**

I've always been a dreamer. I may talk a bit slowly, but I dream huge and amazingly. This poem that my father wrote about me captures perfectly who I was as a child.

Daydreams
by Jerome William Freeman

A child can carry on,
Where we leave off,
With plans and dreams
For yet another generation.

My eight year old son
Captures the spirit properly
As he answers
(In response to an adult's query
about the future)
"I want to be everything."
Me too.
Even Now

Jerome Freeman, SOMETHING AT LAST: Dakota Poetry and Sketches, Penstemon Publishing, 1993. Pg. 12

As a young kid, my parents told me I was the best and who was I to disagree? I lived in happy agreement with them until the fourth grade. However, I'm sure things had been simmering somewhere in my awareness for years. These things reached a boiling point when I transferred from a private school in Sioux Falls to Valley Springs Elementary. Sioux Falls is the biggest city in South Dakota. Valley Springs has a tiny blue water tower and if you walk out from the center of town to the edge you will hit a corn or soybean field within 10 minutes.

PERFECTLY IMPERFECT

*It's January. Outside, snow smothers the
ground. The sky is an unrelenting gray and
it's 20 degrees below zero. Inside my grade
school, I fidget in an uncomfortable child's
desk in Mrs. Olson's class. The old-building
heat is claustrophobic. Above our heads
a swarm of fluorescent lights buzz noisily.
And then, for some reason the realization
happens. Something here is not like the
others. As I look around the room, I'm
puzzled. What could it be? What is different?
Slowly it dawns on me. Oh no! What a
catastrophe! It's me!*

*It's me! And life goes on—kind of. I'm
beginning to realize that I'm not like the
other kids. In gym class, the other boys throw
balls and catch them with ease. Often as not,
these same balls fly right through my hands
or hit my forehead, glasses, chin, or stomach.
It's painful and humiliating.*

*Then, it gets worse. To cope, I decide not to
let on that my voice and coordination not
only bother me, but mortify me. I repeat to
myself, "I hate this! I hate this! I hate this!"
I become skilled at putting on the "Happy
Face"—you know, the one that makes
everyone believe things are peachy, but really
you're dying inside.*

Do you ever put on the "Happy Face?

Fifth grade: I have only one friend here. I can't think of what to say to the other kids. I'm a dork. I imagine the other kids hate me. I figure I'm disgusting.

I develop a crush on a girl in my class. I also chew on my shirt because I'm awkward and nervous. The girl won't give me the time of day.

Sixth grade, I go out for the basketball team. I catch lots of basketballs with my glasses. Miserably, I don't score a point all season; but it's a winning season for the eyeglass shop in town.

Looking back, the teachers at Valley Springs Elementary are heroes in my book, but I didn't appreciate them as heroic at the time. I was just trying to survive.

Do past wounds ever come back to you, when you finally decide to make an effort to express the authentic you?

Right now, I feel it—the concern that I'm not getting this first chapter right. The concern appears as pain in my forehead.

*I'm three years old when I decide to
dive off some playground equipment.
Fortunately, I catch myself with my forehead.
Unfortunately, I am so banged up it calls
for an emergency room visit, but the nurses
won't let my Mother into the treatment room
while they work on me. I'm an only child
accustomed to being by my Mom's side day
and night. This is how I know safety and
comfort in the world. Suddenly, my head is
throbbing, blood is coming out of me and my
Mom is ripped away from me.*

Funny that that experience which is so ancient to
my life, is coming back to me while I try to type my way
through this chapter. Could it be that the same sense
of loss of safety and comfort that was ripped away from
me is returning in my efforts to share who I am with my
readers? As I write, I'm plagued by thoughts of self-doubt
that what I'm writing now isn't important enough to be
in a first chapter. What if no one reads this? What if this
is no good? I was an English major and have a Master of
Fine Arts In Poetry. I should know how to write better for
heavens sakes!

**Generally, the more important the
communication, the more we struggle with trying to
make it perfect.** I notice that I don't experience much
self-doubt when I'm talking about the weather. (You could
argue that I live in San Diego now and there's no weather
to talk about. And that is a fair argument). **Why is this
discussion even important? Because, "stuffing" our truth
down by not communicating what we need and what we**

want out of life can hurt us!

The following fictional scenarios give an idea of what can happen when we refuse to communicate our innermost needs and wants:

The book that is loved in dreams slowly dies when the author abruptly quits after chapter 3 because he doesn't think it's any good. He has every intention of picking it up again, but one excuse leads to another, one year slips into another, and the words the author might have blessed the world with collect dust and might as well be pushing up daisies.

There's been a misunderstanding between two friends. There is hurt. There is pain. They take sometime away from each other to cool off. A few days drag into months and the misunderstanding grows in their minds as they don't talk. Each of them wants to reconcile but can't come up with the perfect words to set things right. A friendship that could have so enriched both of their lives dies a slow death.

A woman is passionate that children living in poverty should have all the benefits other children enjoy. She has a brilliant plan to end childhood hunger in California. She has a long list of groups she wants to speak to in an effort to gain support for her plan. She starts to write her speech, only to pull her hair out as she agonizes over every word. Eventually she quits, convinced that she is not good enough to deliver this message and that somebody much more qualified and more intelligent will come along and deliver the message much better than she could. No one comes along. She dies. Kids go hungry.

Sad, imaginary scenarios. In our fear, we demand perfection in how we express ourselves. Then we can't live up to this standard, because something can always be a little more perfect. Since it's not perfect, we don't express it. When we don't express what is important, we suppress, and that suppression has a tendency to come out sideways in the form of stress, unhappiness, boredom, numbness, anger, rage, pain, or all of the above. Isn't that fun?

Seeking perfection before we communicate or take action is like running a never-ending marathon.

Imagine training hard for a marathon. In fact, you have trained for four months, following your training regimen to a T, getting up at 5 AM so many mornings when you feel like sleeping in. You're proud of what you've accomplished. Now it's race day and everything is going great. Your running partner is the perfect person to pace you and inspire you. The day is just right, sunny and fifty-five and you are feeling strong—the strongest and most powerful you have ever felt in your life.

You and your running buddy pass people left and right. You can't believe your ears when a person at mile twenty-four screams your time. It's so good, and there are just a few more quick miles to go. The finish line is in sight. You are running your final sprint and pulling far ahead of even your running partner. You see the two women holding either side of the finish line sitting in their cars on either side of the road, and you wonder why they're in their cars on such a perfect day.

Then, just as you are within two yards of the finish line, the two women speed off in tandem and the finish line disappears over the hill. You are exhausted so you stop about where the finish line would have been, utterly out of breath. Even though the finish line bizarrely disappeared, and you are exhausted after running a full marathon, you are utterly elated because you finished in record time. In fact, you are on top of the world and feel that you definitely have hit a high-water mark in your life. Then, about a minute later you notice everyone racing past you. How can this be? A volunteer rushes up to you and asks you, "Is anything wrong?" You smile and gasp, "I did so good! I finished the marathon in great time. **I really accomplished my personal best.**"

The volunteer says, "I'm so happy you are all right but I need to tell you that you didn't finish yet. **They decided to move the finish line to mile thirty-one.** If you still are interested in finishing with a good time, you best get going right this minute."

You laugh. "What a funny joke to play on someone who has just run their best marathon. You planned that out so well with the finish holders driving off. This will make a great story to tell all my friends."

The volunteer replies, "I hate to break it to you but it's no joke. The finish line is now at mile thirty-one. **The Judge decided to move the finish line to mile thirty-one. So now the old finish line MEANS ABSOLUTELY NOTHING.** If you stop here, I'm afraid we can't even give you a t-shirt for a finish, because **you didn't finish.**"

Out of control and irate, you scream, "But I ran 26.2 miles! That's the length of a complete marathon." The volunteer says in a very calm voice, "I understand that you **THOUGHT it was the length of the marathon. And it was until about ten minutes ago.** But the Judge changed his mind. Now a marathon is defined as 31.3 miles. A marathon is now 31.3 miles because the judge says it is."

The desire to punch the volunteer out is coursing through your body and with a rush of adrenaline you feel you have the strength, even after running those 26.2 miles. Instead you belt at the top of your lungs, **"But that is so completely UNFAIR."**

The volunteer's voice is rising and becoming assertive. "Now sir, if you don't calm down I'll have to use my walkie-talkie and call security over." So you sit down completely dejected and start to cry. The volunteer softens, waits a few minutes and sits down with you. He tries to explain, "You see **the judge believes in going above and beyond.**"

Luckily marathon judges aren't known for moving the finish line, but **how often do you function as your own judge and keep moving the finish line on your personal best?** We sometimes do this almost reflexively thinking, **"Well I can do just a little better."** Or we cross the finish line and think, **"Well that is JUST NOT A GOOD ENOUGH RESULT** for me to be finished and congratulate myself. Or we see someone else running farther than the point we declared as our finish line, and think if they are running farther, **"I'd better run farther SO I DON'T GET LEFT BEHIND."**

The concept of your personal best can become utterly lost because you never allow yourself a finish line, you never allow yourself a completion point. **Everything you are working on in your personal and professional** life becomes unfinished and you never achieve your best, because it is a point you constantly UNDERMINE by creating your NEW PERSONAL BEST.

Allowing ourselves to do our imperfect best is essential to discovering a fresh path of living. If we demand perfection, we either stuff our words, dreams, hopes and best ideas deep inside because they never are good enough to make the cut of the demands we place on ourselves, or we get things out very, very slowly because we keep second guessing, back tracking, revising, and generally shaking in our "running shoes."

I say "we" as if your journey to becoming comfortable in your own ski will be the same as mine. This of course isn't true unless you are a clone of me. If you are a clone of me, we really need to talk. Mercy me, I hope we can understand each other.

IMPERFECT BEST REFLECTIONS

A Section Just For You

When in your life did you dream the biggest?

What are your fondest memories of this time?

What's a talent, big or small, that you often hide from the world?

What would it be like to offer this talent to the world?

Chapter 11
HAPPILY ORDERED IMPERFECTION

June 22, 2016, 8:54 PM Central Time. I sit here in row 16A on Delta flight 2786 bound for San Diego. There are 28 emails in my inbox, all from today. I have all the Facebook messages in that inbox documented in my daily document ready to get to tomorrow. There are only a few text messages on my phone, all responded to. My voicemail inbox is down to one special voicemail I'm saving.

I just ate a Ritter Sport candy bar. I'm experimenting with non-gluten ways to get my sugar fix. Now my stomach hurts. Once I buy a treat with sugar in it, I've never been good at eating only a fifth, forth or half. As I eat, I like to gain momentum until I consume the whole thing. I'm tired of the intensity of this habit. Starting tomorrow, I'm vowing to have a blatantly sugary snack only every other day.

The departure from Minneapolis is a beautiful dusk takeoff. I see clouds mirrored in a couple of lakes, some well-lit baseball diamonds, and lightning snaking across a distant thunderhead.

Most of my life I was a nervous person. I guess I

hid it pretty well because I didn't get the sense that people thought of me that way. One of my methods for coping with nervousness was to be selectively organized about things I thought I could be good at or that I figured were really important. Then I was disorganized about much of the rest.

As a writer, I convinced myself that disorganization was an important part of my creative process, in much the same way that I now try to convince myself that massive amounts of sugar are important to my enjoyment of life. My speech impediment and coordination differences helped me justify being disorganized about the things that challenged me. After all, I was disabled. So why should I expect organizational excellence from myself?

Order is such a powerful creative force. Successful companies from Walmart, to Honda, to Apple are highly ordered. A frog is more ordered than an ant, since it has a more complex cellular structure. And, a human is more ordered than a frog.

It's four years ago and I'm looking through the glove box of my car when I notice to my shock and dismay that I can't find the registration for my car. I spend much of the next weekend cleaning out my closet. At last, as I dig through yet one more box of chaos, my car's registration appears.

On another occasion, I'm in college and just finished lunch. I place my tray on the conveyor belt, unaware that I've left my new very expensive retainer on the tray. I call my mom to tell her I lost my retainer and she tells me to go find it. I ask the kitchen workers and they point me to ten or more trash bags full of the remains of hundreds of students' lunches. They give me a pair of gloves. I dig through bag after bag of scraps and partially eaten meals. It's tedious and it's gross. After several hours I touch something that feels solid, something that is not a chicken bone. My retainer.

I lived much of my life this way, struggling to keep my head above the disorder I created. At the same time, this disorder saved me time and time again from attempting things that seemed too scary. Selective order and general disorder made up my comfort zone. What time did I have available to ask girls out on dates when I was busy digging through closets full of papers trying to find the important ones? What hours did I possess to join the intramural basketball league, when I was digging through bags of mashed potatoes and gravy trying to find a dental appliance?

I'm like ants and frogs. I'll do what it takes to survive. When I was disorganized, I found survival consumed much more of my time, and left little time for thriving and creativity.

Today, engaging in ordered activities helps me immensely. When I find myself slipping into a negative mood, I turn my energy towards accomplishing items on my "To Do" lists or clearing out my inboxes. These activities focus my mind and help me feel productive. Then, often before I know it, I haven't dipped nearly as low emotionally as if I had either spent time dwelling on my problems or trying to forget them.

I've wanted to be this ordered in my life for years and would often try, but my attempts would just as often end up in "overwhelm mode." Being overwhelmed would cause me to quit. After years of pain and frustration, I've finally figured out that I'm much happier when I work each day with the goal of functional organization, instead of my former pattern of binge organizing, followed by weeks of neglect.

My systems for ordering my life are far from perfect. Even so, these days my email inbox is frequently down to zero. At the same time, the large number of folders with old emails in them remain to be erased or indexed, and I could spend tomorrow exclusively focused on cleaning out and organizing those folders. Or, I could spend another week or two organizing all the documents on my computer, and then attacking all my paper files—and on and on and on into weeks or months of Jason-Freeman-organizational- escapism-towards-organizational-perfection.

But, if I consistently organize past files and folders for ten or fifteen minutes each day, I can make progress and keep up with the rest of my life too. It has taken me thirty years to learn this balancing act. And it's a lesson well learned, as I find that **being ordered enhances my ability to concentrate and be creative. I love that this path is leading me into a life of radiant ability.**

When I wrote the first paragraph of this chapter, I felt uniquely thrilled and concerned—thrilled at what

I've accomplished by becoming more organized, and concerned that I'm coping with turning forty-one by becoming really boring.

It seemed far cooler to be a disorganized, discontented poet raging against the cruel fates that had cast disability upon me before I could even cry my first tear. Now, however, I find I prefer the outward bland awkwardness of being as highly ordered as I can be, to the misery of being cool in my dishevelment.

I'm finding in mid-life the feeling of being disorganized is not relaxing in the least. For me, feeling disorganized leads to feeling nervous; feeling nervous leads to feelings that I shouldn't feel nervous, which leads to guilt; and, guilt makes my sweet tooth the most powerful organ in my body. (Actually, I don't even need guilt to power up my sweet tooth.) This whole cycle saps my energy and makes me less available to spend quality time with people and pursue interests that matter to me.

A huge part of the organizing victory I mentioned at the beginning of the chapter is that I can report these results even though I've been on vacation to see my parents and friends from the Midwest. Amazingly, achieving these organizational results didn't take that much time. The first two days of my visit I spent no time on the computer. The next three days, I spent one to two hours a day. For most of my life, vacation has been an excuse for me to let things pile up while I relax. Plus, I've told myself that I want to spend as much time as possible with family and friends.

One of the fruits of being organized is that it's much easier for me to follow threads. For example, I have an upcoming engagement to speak at the California

Teacher's Summit, which is a chance to impact many teachers and could lead to countless opportunities to speak in schools across the state. This invitation occurred because I met someone at a workshop and then a week later we met for coffee. She connected me with an acquaintance of hers and he and I exchanged emails, followed by a Skype call. Eventually he recommended me to speak at the conference. This whole process started a few months ago. I haven't said or done anything profound in interactions and correspondence that created this opportunity. What it took was responding to emails consistently in a reasonable amount of time. Having a powerful video of my public speaking also helped; but, if at any point in this process, I had not emailed him for two or three weeks, it probably would have been a deal breaker.

I've found that many opportunities come from noticing and acting on small things. In the grand scheme of life, deciding to eat one carrot stick instead of one monster cookie, or deciding to respond to one email instead of ignoring it doesn't seem like a big deal. But change often comes in small spurts.

From the seemingly trivial detail of an acorn, a towering oak grows. Like noticing the clouds reflecting in the lakes as my plane took off. Those clouds and those lakes are small details that are now in this chapter, which doesn't mean a great deal now. But say someday this book is read by millions of people. Suddenly, the tiny detail of clouds being momentarily reflected on a few Minnesota lakes on an evening in June gains more significance.

Everything is bright and beautiful until it's not

IMPERFECT BEST REFLECTIONS

A Section Just For You

What ways of ordering your life bring you the most satisfaction?

Are there any ways you want to bring more order to your life?

Which of these ways appeals most to you?

Chapter III
EVERYTHING IS BRIGHT AND BEAUTIFUL UNTIL IT'S NOT

Have you ever felt less than, or uncomfortably different from, or just plain inadequate?

As all the kids in my kindergarten class at All Saints moved on to first grade, I took a year off of the traditional school track to go to Crippled Children's Hospital and School full-time. The thought was that I would benefit from a year of intense occupational therapy, physical therapy and speech therapy, especially since I was well behind the curve in the areas of speech and gross and fine motor coordination. We were fortunate to have such a school in Sioux Falls as I didn't have to travel to another city for the therapy or live in the dorms, which would have been intolerable for my whole family.

How does a little kid deal with such a detour? I didn't think that much about it. However, I distinctly remember having to go to Crippled Children's in the summer when my friends from All Saints were on a three-month break. I threw a fit over that, seeing the arrangement as distinctly unfair and completely wrong to my young mind.

How did I process transferring from a school

called All Saints to a school called Crippled Children's? (This unfortunate name reflected the prevailing view at the time. Some years later Crippled Children's changed its name to Children's Care.) I didn't consciously give the name a second thought, because I don't think I realized that "crippled" had a negative meaning at that time.

At Crippled Children's, my speech therapist Sheila, my physical therapist Jane and my occupational therapist Barb were wonderful to me. Many of my classmates could not talk at all and were in wheelchairs. I was lucky that my legs could run and my voice could speak. I was lucky that I went home to my folks at night instead of having to live in the dorms like many of the other kids. I was lucky that Crippled Children's had a pool in the basement. All Saints didn't have that.

I continued at Crippled Children's in first grade for half a day, and was mainstreamed into All Saints for the other half day. In second and third grade I went all day to All Saints.

All Saints' main building resembled a pink stone castle and was built around 1884. On our way to chapel in the morning during April, we would pass a crabapple tree radiant with pink blooms. The chapel's magical stained glass windows had light streaming triumphantly through, and the sound of the powerful pipe organ made me love to belt out my favorite hymn—"All Things Bright and Beautiful." The first three lines describe life perfectly:

All things bright and beautiful,
All creatures great and small,
All things wise and wonderful,

http://library.timelesstruths.org/music/All_Things_Bright_
and_Beautiful/

After third grade, I transferred to a public school because All Saints school closed. I changed from schools in Sioux Falls, a town of about 80,000 people, to Valley Springs Elementary School, in Valley Springs, South Dakota with a population of about 350 people on a good day. At Valley I became more and more frustrated with the fact that I felt hopelessly different than the other kids. So, I chose to spend my time competing to prove I was as good as they were.

If I couldn't "talk normal" or "shoot a basketball normal" I would work my hardest to get the best grades. I would prove that I was the smartest kid in class by making my name as the teacher's pet. If my body prevented me from being a jock, I would strike back at fate by not only becoming a nerd, but, by becoming the best nerd Valley Springs Elementary had ever seen. Being a nerd became my armor and sword with which I would slay my disability. I was absolutely determined to fight.

Have you ever been driven by an uncompromising quest to prove your worth as a human being?

That became my plan and it seemed to work for a while. When report cards came out, they looked great. I excelled in math, English, social studies, science, and spelling. I also learned how to dot my I's and cross my T's.

49

My fifth grade English teacher, Mrs. Erickson, contacted my Mom today, wondering if I had plagiarized an assignment. Mom told her proudly, "No, he wrote that." I don't know what the word "plagiarize" means.

I had no idea plagiarize meant to cheat. In my book, everything I did in school had to be by the book. I was driven to prove my worth as a student. I was on an uncompromising quest to prove my worth as a human being and I certainly could not do that by cheating. Life had already cheated me because I wasn't like the other boys. I knew that being cheated hurts and it hurts bad.

Once Mrs. Erickson got word from my mother that I hadn't done that assignment by illegitimate means, she read my work to the class to see if they could guess who wrote it. Most of the class guessed "Jason Freeman" and I could feel myself swell with pride. Even though I couldn't carry on a conversation for over five minutes with any of the girls in class to save my life, a teacher read the words I wrote out loud and heaped praise upon them. This proved I was good for something and proof was what I craved.

The stability of earning good grades, however, couldn't prevent life as I knew it from falling apart. The summer after fifth grade began on an exciting note. A family friend gave me a part time job unpacking inventory at her gift shop. Even to a fifth grader the work was pretty boring, so I started telling people I had a job at the University of Tedium. But, I got to work with the owner's daughter who was my age, and that gave me more practice talking to girls, which I desperately wanted and needed!

Even more importantly, I received a paycheck. Here I was, doing something useful for the world and making money. I felt so grown-up and on-top of my game.

Mom drove me into Sioux Falls, my new ten-speed bike on the bike rack of the car. Then I'd bike around Sioux Falls for a while before work. Being able to pedal around the city on my own represented a number of important things to me, one of which was that I had finally learned to ride a bike! What took most kids a week or two and a few scraped up knees before they were riding confidently, took me a few years. During those years, the stock of Johnson and Johnson went through the roof because my parents were busy buying Band-Aids by the crate to patch up my knees.

This summer was also exciting because my best friend John Gridley IV and I had so much to do. Yep, I had a pronounced speech impediment and he was 4th generation John Gridley. We were the true odd couple. John had severe asthma, and I caught basketballs with my glasses, and we were best friends.

I remember once on a field trip that took us on a long drive from town, three of us boys sat farting and burping in the backseat of my Mom's car. John Gridley IV, however, sat up front in the passenger seat contentedly listening to classical music on his Walkman.

Sleepovers were a big deal, and I loved sleeping over at John's house. He collected old fuse boxes—you know, the kind that are in basements or closets and you never give a second thought to unless the lights unexpectedly go out? Well, John Gridley IV was obsessed with acquiring them. He and I would stay up until all hours of the night working on "projects" and pretending to wire the fuse boxes together. We were odd ducks—very odd ducks—and we loved that we had each other.

Another time, I remember John and I surprising my parents by walking from his house in town to my house in the country—probably an eight mile walk—a long and probably unsafe jaunt for two eight year-old kids. But, we were invincible. Of course John promptly threw up on the carpet once we finally made it to my folks. But we were strong as a team. One night we were sleeping on the front porch at John's house. Suddenly, I awoke in time to see him ablaze in his sleeping bag. I yelled and his Dad came running and put the fire out. John had lined his sleeping bag with some heating wire to keep warm. It really worked!

I so want to keep writing these little charming vignettes from our friendship so I don't have to write this next part.

It's a June day and on a whim, before work, I bike by McKennan Park where John is taking tennis lessons. While he studiously applies himself to his lesson, I wave good-bye and set off for the gift shop and boxes of Christmas ornaments to unpack and price. I continue to unpack ornament after ornament, when my Dad walks into the stockroom.

This is wrong, all wrong. This is a workday for my father. I'm not supposed to see him until dinnertime. He's coming towards me, and tells me that my best friend had been biking

*after tennis, was hit by a car, and that we
should go to the hospital. Does my Papa say
much more during that brief drive? I don't
know. But somehow I know John isn't coming
back. We are at the hospital. The surgeon
comes out of the operating room with tears
in his eyes. John's father, John Gridley III,
totally breaks down.*

*My old All Saints classmates and I sit in pews
at John's funeral. We fish through hymnals
to find the songs we are supposed to sing,
just like we did in chapel every morning at All
Saints. It is all so normal, yet so completely
wrong.*

*Now, not only do I need to be perfect to atone
for my horrendous voice and coordination,
I need to be perfect to avoid dying like my
beloved friend. My oddities seem horribly
stark without his oddities for company. I miss
him so much and there is nothing I can do to
make it better.*

*I quit working at the gift shop because I miss
John. I am scared to ride my bike around
town because of what happened to him.*

I felt so fragile—like I had to be really careful just
to stay alive. I had to be tough, too, and prove to the world
that I was more than a disabled loner. I just had to prove

it, and I was failing. Being the best nerd Valley Springs Elementary ever had seen had done nothing to change the facts that seemed to be crowding around me like well-armed, irate enemy soldiers.

John was gone. All Saints was closed and boarded up. No more pipe organ playing on perfect spring days.

Between the wind and rain and the formidable heat of June, crabapple trees in South Dakota lose their tender blossoms way too fast. That's how I felt. That's exactly how I felt.

Have you ever felt like that crabapple?

At the time there's no words to really describe how it feels. There are just no words. What there is to do is just survive and be as brave as you can be.

IMPERFECT BEST REFLECTIONS

A Section Just For You

Think of a time when you felt uncomfortably different from those around you. What was it like for you?

How did you navigate your way through this time?

Think of an unexpected challenge that came into your life. How did you navigate your way through this time?

Chapter IV
ZITS, CHAOS AND KINDNESS

5:30 AM, September 29, 2016. I wake up 45 minutes before my alarm. My left hand itches between my pointer and second finger. The itch immediately reminds me of the infection I have on my hand. When is it going to go away? I've been taking pills for it and faithfully putting cream on it as the doctor prescribed. I've been trying to do everything right, but it hasn't fully gone away yet. What if it never goes away? What if it continues to get worse and worse and becomes a chronic condition and spreads and I can't control it and, and, and...

For most of my life this thought stream would have flowed until it became bigger and eventually turned into a dismal river of rank cascading doubt, consuming the 45 minutes until my alarm went off and the rest of the day, if not the rest of the week.

But this morning, I caught the stream while it was still a trickle. I directed my attention to the sensation of the itching, instead of putting my energy into making up some cataclysmic story of what the itching could turn into in the future. I paid attention to the feeling in my head instead of my usual hypochondriac-on-steroids thoughts. I paid attention to the sound of cars outside. I set an intention of allowing all the love I could in. I started to breathe more deeply. I fell into a peaceful, happy sleep, and only woke up when my alarm went off.

In seventh grade, I had no idea of how to focus my attention away from the agitated river of doubt, fear, and shame that was coursing through me every day. Fearfully entering puberty, I hungered after the perfection of waking up one morning and suddenly speaking and moving normally. Instead, I would wake up each morning feeling worse about myself.

Have you ever had mornings like that—feeling worse about yourself? I imagine we all have.

Back in the day, I *disabled* my potential by lusting after perfection. In my zealous determination to flee me I became totally un-politically correct with myself.

It's 1989 and seventh grade hits me hard. That year Bobby McFerrin's song, "Don't Worry, Be Happy" is big. I love the sound of the song and the wisdom within it. But I don't yet know how to apply that wisdom to my life.

Have you ever loved the wisdom contained in a work of art or a person, but have not yet been able to apply the wisdom you admire to your own life?

I'm terrified of accidental nuclear war breaking out between the United States and the Soviet Union. I am absolutely sure I SHOULD be writing letters to Congress and the President to stop it from happening. But I'm so nervous and scared I can't even concentrate on that.

At school, no one is bullying me. They don't need to. I'm doing a spectacular job of that all on my own. Besides, nobody understands. I'm as lonely as the Maytag Man on TV. But at least he has a purpose and talks right. I'm good for nothing.

Do you know what it's like to be at war with yourself?

It's the spring of '89, I leave school unannounced, and ride my bike home furiously. I don't notice the spring day, or whether there might have been huge cotton candy clouds floating in a blue sky, or mammoth oaks just beginning to push out tiny leaves, or whether there could have been lilacs in bloom. I'm blind—so blind. I'm in a panic. I write a suicide note without really knowing what it says. I think to myself, "How can I do this? But won't everyone be better off when I'm gone?" I sob and I scream. I'm so confused. I eat half a bottle of aspirin fast and wait.

Luckily, a voice inside of me communicates loud and clear and shouts, "This is not the way." I pick up the phone and call "Help, Help, I can't do this by myself anymore! Help Me! Help Me!"

Our fears can keep us silent. Not only do other people not get a chance to know us, but, tragically we can lose track of ourselves.

WHAT IF I had not called for help?

My parents would have lost a son they loved with all their might. My relatives would have lost a family member whom they loved dearly. All the friends I've had over the years would have lost the chance to be impacted by my presence in their lives and to love me. The world wouldn't have received the benefits from all the work I have done. You would not be reading this book.

Luckily, there is a voice within each one of us that is so much stronger, deeper and wiser than our worst fears about ourselves.

Finding the courage to listen to this voice and love ourselves is vitally important—probably the most important work each of us has to accomplish in this life.

The impact of that call for help washed over me like a soaking rain after a four-year drought. I had been determined to survive by being perfect so people would perceive me as normal. Nothing about consuming half a bottle of pills was perfect OR normal. The inner voice that saved me, and my new-found willingness to communicate changed everything. After that day, I slowly began to open up, first to a therapist and my parents, then eventually to friends and teachers.

Small things contributed to my recovery. I remember the night when Dad and I were sitting at the dining room table and it suddenly occurred to me that I could transfer to a new school for eighth grade. I told Dad my idea with hesitation. After all, I was only a kid and couldn't imagine I had the power to make such a decision. But my Dad liked the idea and I changed schools.

Writing longhand was agonizingly slow for me, so I asked my Mom if I could dictate much of my homework to her. She said yes and took dictation from me hour after hour, night after night. That was an amazing thing for her to do.

In high school, I wanted desperately to drive like the other kids but I feared that my lack of coordination would get me into all manner of accidents. My dad knew I had fears, so he accompanied me as I learned to pilot a car safely. If I were to summarize those car rides in two words, the two I would choose would be "CLOSE CALLS". But my Dad stuck with me and we both lived to tell about it.

Then, when I was coming out of my low points, my Mom listened as I talked about my fears and would always remind me that, "This too shall pass." Mom was right.

Many people take that bicycle ride into utter frustration and anger with themselves at some point in their life. Has this person ever been you?

Has this person ever been someone you love?

How do we encourage each other to call for help at times like these?

What do we do when someone calls us in his or her time of need?

These are important and complicated questions. If you're anything like me, you want to be perfect in your answers to them. But, I found seeking perfection often just drives us further from each other. So we are left to do our imperfect best.

This is what we can do.

This is humanity.

This is love.

This is kindness.

IMPERFECT BEST REFLECTIONS

A Section Just For You

Have you ever been at war with yourself?

What was it like?

What, if anything, helped you to make peace with yourself?

Chapter V

MY BEST SHOT AT NORMAL

High school was enjoyable for me. I had many great guy friends. However, I regretted that I had very few dates. I longed to spend more time with my female peers, so I blamed my lack of poise and luck with women squarely on my disability. Obviously, if I could only talk normally, I would have had girls swirling around me like moths to a porch light. Sometimes the despair overwhelmed me, convincing me that my disability would shut my porch light of attractiveness off permanently.

Other than my frustration and extreme jealousy that many of my male peers had girlfriends and I did not, hanging out with a group of fascinating guys who really enjoyed having me as a friend filled the void. Favorite memories include the many trips on which my parents took me and some of my male friends. The guys appreciated my great sense of humor, and learned that I was a wonderful listener who would ask them question after question to keep them talking. And I discovered that I could keep a conversation going for hours simply by asking questions. I didn't want to reveal that trying to think of things to say made me nervous, or that I saw my life as boring and insignificant, or my fear of not being understood if I talked for too long. If my friends asked me to talk for more than a few minutes about what I really thought and how I really felt, I would quickly ask them a question to focus the conversation back their way.

During those years I developed a friendship with another student, also named Jason, who loved reading and writing poetry. Poetry had fascinated me since childhood because my Dad always greatly enjoyed reading and writing it, and he gladly nurtured my countless early poetry writing efforts. So when I met another Jason who loved poetry, we naturally started sharing our favorite poets and the latest poems we had written with each other.

Who do you share your passions with?

One part of the adventure of living in a country setting, particularly during the summer months, was the never-ending list of work to be done. My parents employed a few of my friends and me to work on our property during summer vacation. We cut down pines with hand-saws, then hauled them to a designated location. When we had enough cut, we would spend a long afternoon loading the branches into a dumpster, while we listened to classic rock on a portable radio. Then we'd prune trees, dig a ditch or two, take up an old barbed wire fence and replace it with new fencing, or build dry stone-walls out of pink quartzite stones. One particularly distressing job was given to my friend Chris and I—burying a cow that was not only dead, but that had been actively decaying for quite some time. I won't go into details, other than to say my face still scrunches up at the memory. To this day, I don't think I've ever had a worse job.

Working outdoors, doing tough manual labor greatly boosted my confidence in what my body could achieve. One of the most fulfilling things to me about this type of work was the ability to see the results of your labor at the end of the day.

Even with the outdoor work and fun friendships, I was not fully out of the disabled woods. In junior high and high school, I developed a habit of refusing to play video games, instead watching my friends play for hours. I assumed I would just embarrass myself if I attempted to play, so instead, I became a "watcher," as my friends engaged in video game battles for long periods of time. I delighted when they beat a level and sympathized when they lost. Living through my friends' skills, I felt that I was taking part in the video game world, but in my own way.

What have been the "disabled woods" in your life?

What have you told yourself you won't be good at for so long that you don't even try?

In retrospect, I recall high school as probably the most "normal" time of my life.

While helping my parents with land work, and participating in various aspects of high school life that were important to me, I was well aware that I would not be working outdoors for the rest of my life. I think my parents probably expected from the day of my birth that I would go to college. Education had been their path to success, so naturally it would be mine. As a grew up, I understood that a kid finished high school and then went on to college. My parents and I shared the assumption that in college, even if I majored in English, I would take all the prerequisites that I needed to apply to med school. Then I would apply, be accepted, complete med school, residency and become a doctor like my Dad.

In high school, I was too young to think about what kind of doctor I wanted to be, but that was OK. I had time to decide. I knew life as the son of a doctor, and assumed I would have the same life. I would fit nicely into that well-defined and prestigious role in society.

With my hand/eye coordination, a career as a surgeon didn't seem too practical. I wouldn't trust myself to operate on a Cabbage Patch Doll. But my Dad specialized in neurology. I assumed that with practice and determination I could do what he did—at least at those times when I felt confident in myself, and didn't crush myself like a saltine cracker under the clenched fist of self-doubt.

IMPERFECT
BEST
REFLECTIONS

A Section Just For You

Who do you share your passions with?

What do you love about sharing your passions with others?

What have been the "disabled woods" in your life?

What have you told yourself you won't be good at for so long you don't even try?

Chapter VI
MISERABLE EXPECTATIONS

I spent most of my life misunderstanding my potential. In seventh grade, I understood that I was horrible, not worthy of friendship or love, utterly certain at the time that I had a complete grasp on the breadth and depth of who I was.

How often do we misunderstand the greatness within us? Can we fault ourselves for this?

Just think about it! How could a caterpillar predict that one day out of its crawling, worm-like life a magical flying creature called a butterfly would appear? It is uncanny how our own brilliance can emerge from places that seem least likely. Often before we discover this brilliance, we flounder, misunderstanding our true capability. This lack of understanding can create painful indecision and a disabling awkwardness in our lives.

My high school years brought great friendships and social growth, but now I had to make a truly serious, life-altering decision—one that would directly affect how I spent the rest of my life. I had to decide what college to attend, and what I would become.

I took the ACT and scored a 23. While that was not the 32 that one of my friends got, it still gave me plenty of choices for college. My parents took one of my friends and me on a trip to tour three private colleges in Minnesota. Going to college away from Sioux Falls and my parents seemed like an interesting idea, but at the end of the day I couldn't imagine myself living even a few hours away from them. I chose to go to Augustana College in Sioux Falls. I was accepted, and I decided that I wanted to live in the dorms rather than live at home with my folks. I wanted, and needed, some independence—just not too much.

The first semester was an adjustment for me just as it was for countless of other college freshmen. Academically, I did well, particularly in calculus and inorganic chemistry—two pre-med prerequisites. I was on track—**So Far So Normal.**

When I registered for second semester classes, I signed up for organic chemistry without thinking much of it. But during my first day of class it became abundantly clear to me that I would have to learn to love organic chemistry an awful lot and devote countless hours to our romance if I wanted to have any hopes of passing the class. However, I intuitively knew during that first week that cultivating a romantic relationship with organic chemistry was not going to happen. Truth be told, I didn't even want to be casual friends with organic chemistry. Actually, it became my deepest and most profound wish to avoid organic chemistry at all costs.

Have you ever been in this position of knowing in your heart early on that you want to break something off?

My intuition won and I flat out dumped organic.

By default this meant that my plans of going to med school instantly dumped me, because organic is an absolute prerequisite for med school. I officially chose to skip out on my best shot at "normal," and soon discovered that in the absence of normal, confusion was more than happy to fill the vacuum.

What's a time in life when you deviated from the path you assumed you would travel? How did that make you feel? Did you, like me, experience a vacuum of confusion, or did something else happen?

In a dizzying short one and a half weeks between the beginning of second semester and officially walking into the Administration Building and dropping organic chemistry, I went from living a life where my future was nicely mapped out along the interstate of success, to gazing out upon a future that was decidedly undecided. Even though I was greatly relieved not to be spending my time studying for organic chemistry tests and floundering through the lab, to say that I had no credible Plan B would be a gross understatement. I felt like I was wandering through a deep overgrown, thorn-bush-laden forest, trying to find anything leading to a clear path.

What would have happened if I had just soldiered my way through organic? I don't know. It's impossible to know how the paths we choose not to go down would have turned out.

There's a voice within each one of us that is so much stronger, deeper and wiser than our worst fears about ourselves. I had heard that voice speak to me once before. Looking back on that college decision today, I realize that I listened to that voice again, just as I had done in seventh grade, and as my Grandpa Francis Cloud Schellinger was fond of saying, I made a good move.

However, when I was actually wandering the deep woods of my first college crisis with so many trusted career landmarks quickly disappearing, I was in the land of major confusion. Had I made a courageous choice that would eventually lead me where I wanted to go? OR had I just made a devastatingly selfish and cowardly choice that would ruin my life? I surely didn't know the answer to these questions.

Have you ever been so uncertain about a choice you've made?

My parents and I both wanted me to recover some sense of a normal career path to cope with this uncertainty. We entertained different options. One week I decided to pursue nursing. The next week I chose to get the education necessary to become a physician's assistant. I expressed a brief excitement about a career path as Doctor of Osteopathic Medicine. But then again, maybe I could be a psychologist?

For a short time, I would do the work to get the education necessary to pursue whatever career path I happened to be interested in at that moment. But within a few days my resolve would crumble. I felt like a failure before I began anything. Breaking the sad news to my parents, we went back to square one of Jason Freeman, Career Planning 101.

Finally, I settled on following in my Mother's footsteps and acquired a Social Work major to compliment the English major I had been determined to get since the first day of my freshman year. For a time I had a destination, and career confusion subsided. But as I progressed through the major, I discovered that I didn't want to pursue a career as a Social Worker.

If we are lucky, teachers come into our lives to alert us that the limited view we have of ourselves doesn't represent a permanent reality. But, these teachers don't always come in the form we expect.

It's 1999. I've milked the shelter of college for all it is worth. I have two majors to show for it—English and Social Work. Unfortunately, all that education hasn't removed my major lack of self-confidence.

A month before graduation, I go to see a career guidance counselor. He suggests I apply for disability. On one level, I'm deeply offended by the idea. On another level, he simply echoes and confirms my worst fears.

Is this what I have to look forward to now— applying for position after position, only to have every employer say, "Jason we really like your personality, but unfortunately you won't be a good fit?" Then like the guidance counselor suggested, deeply ashamed again, will I apply for Social Security Disability? Will I try to amuse myself on disability for the rest of my life? Will I become miserably stressed out from having no purpose and doing nothing of use?

Luckily, life quickly proved that guidance

counselor and my worst fears wrong. After unsuccessfully applying at a taco shop and a grocery store, I got an interview for a job at an agency that served adults with a variety of special needs. The position was for part-time direct service work in a home for twelve adults, age 20 to 60, with varying disabilities from Down syndrome, to traumatic brain injury and autism.

I got the job and was thrust into a most unexpected adventure. My part-time hours were 4 PM to 9 PM on Friday, followed by 9 AM Saturday through 8 AM on Sunday. At first, this appeared to be a dream come true. The 23-hour Saturday to Sunday shift seemed kind of long, but my supervisor pointed out that, "You are young." Besides, how much work could it really be hanging out at some group home for 23 hours? More importantly, I would have five days off to write, walk around town and pine after the woman I had a surplus of romantic interest in.

It only took one weekend for me to discover that the job involved much more than hanging out at some people's house. It involved learning the communication styles of 12 residents, each of their communication styles being entirely different.

One man from a foreign country communicated with only ten English words, and he used those words progressively more emphatically until you figured out what he wanted. Another resident had a candy obsession. He called candy "lop," though we never learned why. He constantly followed me around saying, "I want lop." "When do I get lop?" "lop!" "Lop!" "LOP!!!" Relief only came when it was time to take him to the gas station to get him candy. He didn't say anything for the two and a half minutes it took him to stuff all the candy into his mouth. Then he would smile with satisfaction and start right up again, "I want Lop." "When do I get lop?" "lop!" "Lop!" "LOP!!!"

In addition to trying to navigate the vast variety of communication styles of the residents, I was part of a group of staff responsible for helping residents with various hygiene needs and aiding some of them with bathing. We also cooked three meals a day for the house, made the kitchen spotless afterwards, passed out meds, vacuumed, sanitized the bathrooms, dusted, did laundry, encouraged the residents to help when appropriate, helped calm them down when they were irritable, and took them out shopping and to fun activities about town.

Things rarely went as planned. Often drama would ensue. Between the different communication styles, and radically differing likes and dislikes of the residents, there was a constant variety of dramatic adventures. Not to mention that each staff member, including me, added their own communication styles and personalities into the mix. Wow! There simply was an overabundance of activity going on most of the time.

Eventually, I became a floater, moving around to all the different houses in the agency, assisting some of the more independent residents who basically needed someone to take them grocery shopping or remind them to take their meds. Then I also helped people needing assistance with everything. They needed to be fed, transferred from their wheelchair to bed and back, help with bathing—and no matter what their need, I learned from each of them.

However, even after a decade of external

praise from the staff and residents, in my heart I still misunderstood who I was and the merits of what I had to offer the world. I remained unmarried, not even dating. To make matters worse, I could have won the gold trophy for being the most stressed out person in the U S of A. I was highly gifted at worrying until the cows came home, while they were sleeping, and then worrying while they awoke the next morning. This level of stress simply was not sustainable. Something had to change.

Have you ever felt so ready for a change in your life, but had no idea how to make it happen?

I held this job for a decade, and only gave my notice to them because I was ready to pursue new things. I will forever be grateful to the people who lived in the houses where I worked. They taught me about the power of embracing life and being exactly who I am. My coping strategy had been one of trying to hide so much of the real me. By being themselves, they challenged me to come out of hiding and move beyond being mad at life for not making me a heartthrob or a jock. They challenged me to let go of my super nerd crutch. They challenged me to finally decide to be exactly who I was and to fully commit to doing my imperfect best by living life as fully as I knew how. I strive to incorporate their profound lessons into my life to this day.

Who have your unexpected teachers been and what did they teach you?

IMPERFECT BEST REFLECTIONS

A Section Just For You

When do you come closest to understanding the greatness within you?

Have you ever been in the position of knowing in your heart early on that you want to break something off?

What did you do next?

What's a time in life when you deviated from the path you assumed you would travel?

How did that make you feel?

Did you experience a time of confusion, or did something else happen?

Have you ever felt so ready for a change in your life but had no idea how to make it happen?

Who have been your unexpected teachers?

What did they teach you?

Chapter VII
EXPANDING VISIONS

Eight years ago I had a vision of speaking to forty-thousand people at Grant Park in Chicago. There's a part of me that still has to catch up to my grandiose visions.

Another part of me wants to cling furiously to the dimensions of the life I live now. It is a life where the opportunity to speak to 800 two summers ago had me anxious for three weeks prior to, and four weeks after the event because, naturally, I thought I had done an absolutely awful job.

This part of me that is perfectly aligned with the life I live now is campaigning for the status quo and campaigning hard. This part of me finds it a bit hard to face the idea that my career and my life are rapidly expanding.

It reminds me of the time in college when I signed up to go on a January J-term trip to Israel. Soon after signing up, I promptly came up with the fear that touring around Israel could be unsafe. There could be terrorism. If I went, I could be kidnapped or murdered or worse. (Actually I'm not sure what could be worse.)

I decided to get out of it and told the person that I registered with that I no longer wanted to go, even though a woman I had a serious crush on was going. I ended up staying on campus that January taking music appreciation. The weather was frigid. Since music through the ages isn't a primary passion of mine, the class was somewhat interesting, somewhat boring.

My experience that January was lukewarm (at least when indoors), so-so, a combination of staying in my comfort zone and regretting it. I spent that month placating fear instead of risking the wonder of adventure. By staying home, I also avoided the hypothetical terror that the woman I had a crush on might ignore me the whole time we were traveling.

Going to Israel would have been a decision to play center court. Instead I chose the familiar. Staying on my college campus allowed me to retreat high up into the bleachers of my life where I could hide my awkwardness. High up in the bleachers, there was less chance of "basketballs" hitting me in the face. I could vicariously enjoy others trekking down the path towards finding what they most wanted in life, without running the risk they took of getting seriously lost along the way. By not attempting to go places in life at least I would always know where I was.

That January previewed what backing away from a life of challenges would feel like. I learned more about keeping myself busy and feverishly outwitting boredom, but that wasn't the knowledge I craved. All month, some wisdom within me that I tried to numb out and not acknowledge knew that my best life would have been on an adventure in Israel. This wisdom knew in truth that I would have preferred the edge-of-your-seat trial and error of exploring a distant sacred land to walking around a familiar campus where I couldn't get lost even if I was blindfolded.

During that month, I discovered that sometimes the path of least resistance can be bitter cold, both literally and figuratively. Maybe my settling that January taught me to embrace the challenge of constantly rediscovering who I am, instead of sticking to old definitions of me where I always end up feeling awful about myself and my actions correlate to this feeling.

But still, this continual rediscovering almost always seems to bring up fear for me. Most often—almost miraculously—I find "evidence" to cling to the old definitions. For example, a few weeks ago I went on Google to learn the correct pronunciation of cerebral palsy because I have a habit of pronouncing it incorrectly. My search brought up a link to a website about the pronunciation. Then right below it I noticed a headline that said something like, "The life expectancy of people with cerebral palsy is 30 to 70." This headline caught my attention to say the least. (The Internet can be so terrifying.)

I called up my dad, who is a neurologist, to ask him what he thought of it. He said the headline didn't apply to me. It applies to people with more severe cases of cerebral palsy. He's a doctor. His explanation made sense. It aligned with the fact that none of the doctors I've ever seen have said anything about me having a limited life expectancy. Still, I created a stubborn thought that goes something like, "What if my Dad and all the other doctors are just trying to shelter me from the truth?"

Such a thought is fear of success in action. I have zero evidence to support this thought, but much evidence that I'm becoming more successful. Recently in Houston, I gave my best speech yet at the Habitude Warrior Conference. Then the day after the exhilaration of my speech, I received the "Above and Beyond" award for the conference. Did I mention that the conference included thirty other speakers, most of them much more well-known than I?

Success, for me, most often stirs up fear-filled thoughts, which, if followed, most often lead me down a rabbit hole, because they represent the emotion of fear and not the most powerful future that can be created. I've fallen down this rabbit hole countless times.

When I identify disruptively stubborn thoughts like these for what they are, breathe with them and give them space, I have the freedom to move towards the success I truly desire. This is a solution that I practice daily.

IMPERFECT BEST REFLECTIONS

A Section Just For You

What's the grandest vision you have for your life?

What do you love about this vision?

Is there a time when you canceled plans that excited you because of fear?

What did that feel like?

What do you do to calm yourself when you have distressingly stubborn thoughts?

Chapter VIII
PILGRIMAGE TOWARDS SUCCESS

What inspires us to turn the chains that bind us into the fuel that drives us?

My parents are wise, and like many kids I've been known to strenuously debate their wisdom from time to time, actually a great many times to times. One of their spot-on pieces of advice to me was that I should consider getting a master's degree in something. However, for years after college, I ignored their advice, determined to get a master's degree in nothing. After all, five years of college had been enough for me. I was tired. Besides what if I completed all the work necessary to acquire a master's degree and then didn't use it? Furthermore, could I even succeed at an attempt to get a master's degree with my speech impediment and coordination differences?

I've noticed that when I'm afraid to move forward, my disability tends to become much more disabling, at least in my mind.

Have you ever noticed a time when you have amplified your weaknesses as an excuse to avoid moving forward?

One day a mutual friend tells my parents that she applied for a low residency Master of Fine Arts in Poetry program in Nebraska. She gives my parents information about it. I look it over and discover that one of my favorite poets of all time, Ted Kooser, is on the faculty. The opportunity to further engage in my love for writing poetry, plus to potentially work with Ted Kooser, in addition to finally satisfying my parent's desire for me to further my education inspires me to at least apply. I have no expectations that I will actually be accepted, which will serve as more evidence that I'm not fit for grad school. But by applying, I can tell my parents that I at least tried. See my strategy? Pretty ingenious, if I do say so myself. I've learned from years of practice that being strategic makes not going for my best in life so much easier.

A few weeks later I receive a letter in the mail with the University of Nebraska Omaha logo on the envelope. I open it, and to my ambivalent surprise I have been accepted to start the next semester. Fortunately, sometimes, our best-laid plans for mediocrity are for naught.

My position as a floater at my group home job in Sioux Falls provided the perfect opportunity to pursue this MFA, as it afforded a great deal of flexibility in terms of setting my schedule. Since my graduate program was "low residency," flexibility was an absolute necessity. Low residency, by the way, means that my classes would convene in Nebraska for two weeks at the beginning of each semester, after which we would each return home and work long-distance with one professor as a mentor for the rest of the semester.

Once I got started, I ended up loving the program.

The two weeks in Nebraska each semester were like a splendid camp for adults. Instead of meeting on a college campus, the faculty and students met at an elegantly cozy, rustically decorated resort in Nebraska City. This was a fairly small MFA program, so more than just school colleagues, the students and teachers all felt to me like extended family. The course work was challenging and inspiring. The friendships were deep.

IMPERFECT BEST REFLECTIONS

A Section Just For You

Have you ever noticed a time when you amplified your weaknesses as an excuse to avoid moving forward? How did you do this?

What did it feel like?

What inspires you to turn challenges into fuel that propels you forward?

Chapter IX
ROMANCE

I posted this on social media once, "I might never get married and at this point I am OK with that. The single life has a great deal of beauty to it. But, who knows? I might get married someday, and I'm OK with that too. Married life also has a great deal of beauty to it. Either way, life is full of the magnificent."

Inspiration struck to write the below poem as I think about what it means to be awkwardly awesome.

Up To You
by Jason Freeman

It's up to you to unlock
the door to self-love
for yourself.

The simple truth
is no one else can.

Ten years ago, if I had seen a poem like this it would have frustrated the heck out of me because I felt so thoroughly locked out of love for myself. I was determined that I would love myself ONLY IF the sound of my voice improved drastically, and ONLY IF my coordination differences "healed." Moreover, I would love myself ONLY IF I found my soul mate, because ONLY "she could complete me." "You complete me" was a romantic line in the movie Jerry Maguire, but I understood it to mean that a soul mate would bandage and soothe the painful lack of love I had for myself. ONLY THEN could I finally build a love for myself upon the foundation of her love for me.

To my way of thinking, finding a soul mate would provide the key to release the self-love I had kept locked away from myself most of my life. **Why are we so afraid to love ourselves?**

Cut to the chase translation: My romantic life hasn't been at all like the fairytales. ANY OF THEM!

My journey of romantic exploration started at age eight and since then has rarely adhered to plan. A huge part of my healing journey has been to return to a truth my parents told me as a kid when they said, "You are the best."

I think I struggled so long and hard to find love for myself because I expected it to come as some grand moment where I finally found the hidden key and unlocked that grandiose door I had kept shut all my life. Instead, I discovered that self-love is an act much more akin to the continual nature of breathing, rather than some huge, earth shattering epiphany.

I'd like to share a few stories with you. From fourth grade into my thirties, I fell in love very easily. I would look to girl after girl, then woman after woman to complete me. For example, sometime after college I fell hard for a woman.   Oh Wow, I loved her! I wanted to spend the rest of my life with her, but found out fairly early on in my relationship with her that she was gay and in the process of coming out, which seemed much more challenging ten years ago in the Midwest.

For years—like five or six if I'm honest—I held out hope that she would discover that she loved me romantically. In actuality, she helped me to emerge as comfortable in my own skin. At the same time, I helped her to come out and become fully comfortable in her identity as a gay woman. We both had our work cut out for us. We were unlikely teachers for each other, but we taught each other essential life lessons. She eventually found the soul mate of her dreams and married her. I participated in that ceremony by reading a poem for them.

Actually, truth be told, she wasn't the only woman I fell in love with who turned out to be gay. Over a period of ten years, I fell in love with three gay women! A DECADE of my life spent being in love with women who couldn't reciprocate my love in a romantic way. WHY? WHY! For years I played the victim and told myself things like, "It's just bad luck that I fall in love with gay women," or "My disability somehow makes it so I can't fall in love with a straight woman." Frustration reigned during that decade.

But, don't get me wrong. I have had real life romantic experiences, like the time I made a foolish move in, of all places, a Walmart parking lot.

In college, I had a huge crush on "Katie." She had a boyfriend, but there always seemed to be drama in their relationship, so I held out hope. One day we went to Walmart together to run errands. Let me confess earlier that day I had whined to a friend that I really wanted something more to happen with Katie and my friend encouraged me to make my feelings known in some small way. So here I was, with full heart palpitations and the object of my heart's desire in the Walmart parking lot. So, what did I do? I asked her if I could kiss her on the cheek. She awkwardly approved my request, and my lips stumbled toward her face. As we drove away from the store together, Katie proceeded to explain the concept of a platonic friendship to me.

It has become increasingly clear to me that in my self-loathing I wouldn't have found the kind of deep loving, romantic connection I craved. At the time, I **thought this was a case of mistrusting my love interests, but I now realize that this was a profound and painful case of mistrusting myself.**

These women taught me many lessons about deep and glorious friendship. Writing this now I see that they also helped me make the journey from feeling miserable in my awkwardness to feeling awesome in my awkwardness. They did this by setting strong boundaries for me again and again. They didn't permit me to get lost in all the layers of loving them romantically. Instead, **they held up mirrors again and again through which I could see myself more and more clearly.** These mirrors helped me establish an awkwardly awesome orientation towards myself and come into my own as a man who loves himself.

Rest assured, romantic scenarios are something I still aim to improve.

This is all well and good because I've learned that the process of going from miserably awkward to awkwardly awesome involves continually evolving my understanding of myself—and isn't that what life is about—a constant evolution of self?

IMPERFECT BEST REFLECTIONS

A Section Just For You

What are three things you have discovered in the process of learning to love yourself?

What are three things you have discovered in the process of learning to love others?

Chapter X
WHO DO YOU TRUST

How did I learn to trust who I was?

By slowly starting to act in trustworthy ways toward myself.

I can identify important moments in my journey towards trusting myself on a deeper level. However, I initially resisted the wisdom of these moments and only later did I begin to incorporate this wisdom into my life.

My friend Paul and I loved the power of words and ideas. So one day he suggested we start The Sioux Falls Metaphorical Society. We were the two founding members and after two years the only members. Our recruitment efforts were unfocused and half-hearted to say the least. During one of our meetings, Paul mentioned that he thought yoga would help me with flexibility and enhance my chances of getting a girlfriend. Looking at him aghast, I thought to myself, "But Paul, I don't do yoga and I'm not about to start!"

A few months later, as a last minute decision, I went on a driving trip with Aunt Ann to Montana. While there, I saw my other Aunt Ann and Uncle Bill. (Yes, I have two Aunt Anns who live in Montana.) My self-confidence at this time was as brittle as the parched grass on Mt. Sentinel towering above Missoula, Montana.

Talking with Uncle Bill, for some reason I proudly told him about my almost fanatical habit of regularly drinking Coca-Cola to the tune of two to three servings a day. He responded with some powerful stories about the damage Coke can cause and suggested I give it up right away. Like Paul, he also suggested I try yoga.

I thought a good deal about what Uncle Bill said, recalling my many decisions to give Coke up in the past, which never stuck. I always had rationalized my way out of my commitment. My good intentions meant nothing because I couldn't trust myself. This lack of trust imbued many areas of my life. Would yoga help? Come on now! Anyone could see how my body moved. Yoga would only add to my embarrassment, distract the other students, and create extra work for the teacher.

So, I decided to give up Coke!

Within two months, I had drastically reduced my Coke consumption. A few months later I drank my last Coke and haven't had one since. Now I get water out of fountain pop machines all the time, and haven't the slightest desire to cheat and put Coke in my glass.

A huge part of the pain of being miserably awkward was that nagging feeling that I couldn't trust me to keep commitments to myself to improve my life. I could talk a good talk, even with my unique voice, but at the end of the day I would go against my own words of wisdom.

Do you ever go against your own words of wisdom?

I felt so much better not habitually drinking Coke

each day. Secretly, I also hoped that giving up Coke might save me from having to awkwardly engage in some group exercise like yoga. In high school, I ran cross-country and track, but beyond that had avoided group exercise and competitive sports like the plague. Considering that I caught basketballs with my glasses in sixth grade and threw a shot put backwards during a track meet in seventh grade, I just knew competitive sports and group exercises were not for me. This was absolute truth in my book.

But, occasionally in my life I've become so desperate that I rebelled against my absolute truths. In this case, the rebellion came less than six months after I gave up Coke. January 22, 2008 felt like one of the worst days of my life. I had just received my M.F.A. in Poetry a degree I had worked so hard for and devoted two years of my life to acquiring. I loved what I had learned, but I just didn't want to teach, and let me tell you the pickings are mighty slim as a professional poet. In my experience, life feels especially out of control when you give something your all, achieve the desired result, but still feel unhappy because nothing much has changed after the result has been achieved.

So, here I had my MFA, with no prospects for a job as a poet, and the only thing left for me to do was to keep working my group home job. While I loved so many aspects of the job, frankly I was burnt out.

To add insult to injury, in spite of all of my education, I still hated the sound of my voice, still felt disabled, still was totally stressed out and still didn't have a clue about how to cope with real life. I recall feeling as stuck as a hyena struggling in quicksand in my basement apartment on Summit Avenue in frozen Sioux Falls, South

Dakota as my brain spun around and around and around and around about this stuff.

Do you ever do that? Do you ever find yourself thinking about the same depressing stuff over and over again and getting nowhere? How do you handle it?

I remember being confused, frustrated and miserable, even though I didn't want to admit this to myself. I wouldn't understand this term until much later, but **I felt this way because I wasn't listening to my "inner wisdom."** Instead I listened to all the nonsense in my mind. Something had to change. **Something simply had to change!**

I put on my heavy winter coat, stocking cap and gloves. I took a walk down to the Sioux Falls YMCA and signed up for a monthly membership with the intent of using it so I could try the yoga classes. **Something had to change.**

Can you picture a guy who can barely walk a straight line going to his first yoga class? Can you imagine a guy who feels horribly uncoordinated, ashamed of his body, and unattractive doing something so uncharacteristic? It made no sense, but I did it anyway.

A voice inside my head said, "Dude you're crazy", but **something had to change.** My inner bully repeatedly screamed, "You will never be able to do yoga", but **something had to change.** My survival instinct pleaded, "Are you kidding me," but **something had to change.** All the voices saying I couldn't do it were in my head shouting, "Jason you will fail horribly and make a fool of yourself." I didn't care anymore. **Something had to change.**

I don't know what you are going through right now, but **you might be having that same feeling.**

Has your inner wisdom ever told you something has to change? How have you responded to this message?

I'm here to tell you that positive, nourishing change is possible for you.

In spite of all my years of accumulated doubts about my abilities to get through a group exercise class without looking like a blazing red sore thumb, I quickly found that I loved yoga. I loved simply being quiet and moving with my classmates to the teacher's cues. I loved that teachers offered me modifications as I needed them so I would be safe as I progressed through the class. I loved learning how to breathe deeply and develop much deeper concentration. And—surprise of surprises—I found that I utterly adored doing balancing poses (and am pretty good at them). I also shocked myself with my willingness to go to class after class, until now I'm going to class many days a week on a consistent basis.

One day during class I saw a fellow student kicking up into a handstand against the wall. I looked at him, then looked away, thinking to myself, "I'll never be able to do that because I'm disabled. Handstands are for able-bodied people." Well, once again I proved myself wrong—another surprise of surprises! Through years of practice, I've now done countless handstands against the wall!

I love how yoga has transformed the way I experience life. The practice has helped unravel my story of disability and transform it into a story of ability—one breath at a time. Yoga continually brings flexibility to areas where I used to be painfully inflexible. The flexibility of yoga empowers me to create a new daily reality in which I live and breathe the experience of being fully able.

About six months after I began taking yoga classes at the YMCA one of teachers, Jill, walked into class and announced that she and her husband, Dan, had decided to start a Laughter Yoga Club. Inspired by my success with trying regular yoga, I took the leap to try this new thing too.

And just what is "Laughter Yoga" you might ask?

> *"Laughter yoga (Hasyayoga) is a practice involving prolonged voluntary laughter. Laughter yoga is based on the belief that voluntary laughter provides the same physiological and psychological benefits as spontaneous laughter. Laughter yoga is done in groups, with eye contact and a playful attitude between participants. Forced laughter soon turns into real and contagious laughter."*
>
> (https://en.wikipedia.org/wiki/Laughter_yoga)

In Laughter Yoga one laugh leads to another. So, I joined the club and before I knew what happened, I had become a certified Laughter Yoga Leader slated to speak at the All American Laughter Yoga Conference in Estes Park, Colorado.

You know those times when you are so tired of the way things are going that you take a courageous leap forward?

*It's the day of my talk, **I'm terrified, but trying not to act it.** What if the audience doesn't like what I have to say? What if half of them get up and leave? What if? What if? What if.....?*

*I arrive at the venue for the Laughter Yoga conference and I'm met by a full wall of windows presenting a view of majestic mountains. Stripes of light parade through the Rocky peaks. The first thing I do is kick off my shoes. Hey, I'm speaking at a national conference, and comfort has to be my first priority. Having my shoes off somehow emboldens me, so **I decide to set aside my notes for the day and speak from my heart,** sharing what I truly believe in front of a room packed with people. **The results are magic.***

To this day, I'm so thankful for the love with which that audience listened to me. **Right then and there, it dawns on me that I had gotten it all wrong.** Could it be? **Could it possibly be that The Voice I had hated and that embarrassed me my whole life, in fact, makes me a master communicator?**

Dare I admit this?

Imagine what it's like to finally love The Voice?

Once I recognized this gift that I never realized I possessed, I knew I HAD TO share it—not only share it, but get rich quick by sharing it. The determination to share my gift hasn't left me. The get rich quick part hasn't happened, yet. But I have discovered that much more important than getting rich quick is discovering the path you truly want to take in life and then trusting yourself to travel that path.

As I began walking down this path, I realized that while I dearly loved living in Sioux Falls from the age of 3 to the age of 34, I wanted to move somewhere bigger. I believed that there would be more opportunities for business, yoga and to meet single women. Once I realized this and finally worked up the courage to do it, the question became where to move? I narrowed the options down to Minneapolis or San Diego. But darn it, I couldn't decide between the two. Then one of my wonderful friends finally helped me to make the decision.

> *One February evening Dan and I are walking in McKennan Park in Sioux Falls. It has been a long, brutal prairie winter. On that night, it's still cold. It's still windy. There's still snow and ice on the ground.*

> *I say, "Hey Dan, I'm thinking of moving to either Minneapolis or San Diego."*

> *Dan looked around at the chilly, bleak winter night and said something like, "Think about it!"*

I thought about it, but not too long. By July of that year with my Honda Accord loaded to the brim with stuff for my freshly rented San Diego apartment, I set out from

Sioux Falls to begin my journey from snowy winters to palm trees and the Pacific Ocean.

I had at last discovered my path and the ability to trust myself as I proceeded down it. I continue to discover more of this path and more about my ability to trust myself everyday.

Maybe if I had gone to a yoga class before I had successfully given up Coke, I wouldn't have been able to honor my commitment to it. Maybe yoga would have become just another good thing that I wanted to draw into my life but then forgot about when it became too challenging. **The ability to commit to things we love gives power to our lives.** Once I felt I had more power over my life, I became able to love the awkwardly awesome one-of-a-kind person that I am.

Now, am I perfect about following through when I commit to something? No, not at all. Do I, for example, have the perfectly healthy diet? Yes, if the perfectly healthy diet includes monster cookies, taco shop burritos and following other food whims of debatable merit. Otherwise, no, not at all.

I've found that **I don't have to be perfect at committing to things to be successful. I've found that I don't have to be perfect at my diet to feel the most healthy I ever have in my life.** As far as my diet goes, it's been a gradual process of becoming more aware of the input, letting go of those things that are damaging and adding more of the things that make me feel vibrant.

To me, **feeling complete in my awkwardness has nothing to do with being perfect. I simply need to do my imperfect best.**

When I was miserably awkward, I tried to do everything perfectly. I tried to plan out my life so it would be without a flaw. Armed to the hilt with the perfect plan, I believed whenever I went into action that I should only be satisfied with achieving perfect results. It finally dawned on me that the only possible way to achieve perfect results was to keep planning and never act.

Then the circular thinking began. When I learned that perfection was impossible, I'd give up. When I gave up, I wouldn't trust myself. When I didn't trust myself, I would project this distrust onto my relationships with others. Yes, it was a vicious cycle.

The joy of life comes not from waiting for the perfect day to live, but from doing our imperfect best each day.

Do I still want a girlfriend? Oh yes! Do I still want to get married? Possibly! But, now I don't want either of these things at the expense of feeling complete in myself—complete in my magnificent, awkward awesomeness. **This attitude represents continual major growth for me and for that I am deeply grateful.**

I used to hope for huge breakthroughs, like walking into Burger King and suddenly meeting the woman of my dreams, or suddenly networking with that contact who would get me booked for consistent speaking gigs at $10,000 a pop, or suddenly being healed of my speech impediment and coordination differences. Suddenly! Suddenly! Suddenly!

Yes, SUDDENLY sometimes happens and it can be very exciting. But in the meantime, we have our daily lives. We have daily opportunities to feel good about ourselves, daily opportunities to do things we love, daily opportunities to practice again and again honoring our commitments to ourselves and to others. If we have a chance of feeling complete in our lives I strongly believe we will find it in our day-to-day existence.

Life presents us with opportunities to love ourselves breath by breath, hour by hour, day by day. Don't allow those opportunities to pass you by.

IMPERFECT BEST REFLECTIONS

A Section Just For You

What have been three important milestones on your journey of learning to trust yourself?

Do you ever go against your own words of wisdom?

What does that feel like?

Do you ever find yourself ruminating about the same depressing ideas over and over again and getting no where?

When you notice this, how do you handle it?

Has your inner wisdom ever told you something has to change?

How did you respond to this message?

Have you ever found an appreciation for something that you used to dislike about yourself?

What was that experience like for you?

Chapter XI
TURNING THE CORNER

It has taken me a lifetime to appreciate that losing some oxygen at my birth was a miracle. From my vantage point today, I see that my voice and coordination have been invaluable resources as I've gone for my heart's desire of creating my life in a unique way.

There can be miracles even in the circumstances that seem most challenging to us. *Sometimes these miracles are well-hidden and clouded by hurt, anger, disappointment and confusion. The process of discovering the miracles can take a long time, sometimes even a lifetime, but from my perspective it's so worth it.*

(One of my social media posts, 2016)

I'm at what, for me, is addiction central, the Corner Bakery Cafe, Mission Valley, San Diego, CA. I found this spot within months of moving to San Diego six years ago. Almost immediately I discovered that they had monster cookies. My second discovery came minutes later, when I bit into one and quickly surmised that these cookies bring M&M's, massive amounts of sugar and gluten together in a combination that I find incredibly pleasing both to my taste buds and my inner rebel.

When a food has the word "monster" before it, it probably isn't health food. There's no monster tofu delight, no monster rice cakes, no monster five lettuce salad. Monster seems to be reserved for foods with the special power to release the inner deviant in me who has absolutely no interest in obeying the health authorities who say excess sugar and gluten are bad for you. This inner deviant wants to shout from the Corner Bakery Cafe roof top, "You health authorities just ain't no boss of me" as I eat four huge Monster cookies and triumphantly drink a shot of ---- water, yeah, water from my Camelback canteen. Yes, alas, as I've mentioned before I've permanently given up Coke. What a sad day that was for my inner deviant!

After I discovered my monster cookie pal, I proceeded to drive 15 minutes from my home to Corner....ahh, most everyday. In my prime, I would get two daily monster cookies and knew all the Corner staff as if they were grade school chums. A while back, I cut back to one monster cookie a day with relative success.

Today as I write this, I'm eating a bowl of chili, and later I will get a club panini because I've decided to give up things that are blatantly sugary. So far, my inner deviant seems to be at relative peace with my decision. How can this be after a lifetime of rejoicing in countless varieties of things with high sugar content?

At least part of the answer lies in my discovery fairly early in life that I strongly dislike being bored. Thus, after a lifetime of feasting on blatantly sugary things, my habit has become, well, highly predictable.

Likewise, for much of my life, I was seriously

addicted to being a creative drifter. As a creative drifter, I might have written down the title *Awkwardly Awesome* in a notebook and under it, four or five ideas to expand upon the book. I would have gotten the creative rush from coming up with something from my very own brain that had so much potential. Yes, this type of creative rush was much like a sugar rush. Fast. Powerful–like the momentary feeling of being on top of the world instead of being confind by rules like gravity and the movement of the seasons.

After that creative rush eventually wore off, I would move onto my next idea, probably something totally different like calling myself a Story Expansion Expert and Reviser (a SEER for short) and starting a coaching business to help my clients expand their story, and thereby expand their bottom line. (By the way, I just came up with that one and kind of like it.) Then I would be hot on being a SEER for a few days before I moved on to something else.

I found it irresistibly tempting to just keep drifting from idea high to next idea high to the next, rationalizing that it was harmless. I found this process of drifting to be absolutely thrilling. I felt clever, creative, in the flow, alive.

Eventually I also felt miserable. I would create beautiful ideas, but then stop before much could come of them. In bookstores, I would behold countless examples of people who did so much more than write down a neat title and a few witty ideas. In my inbox, I would get emails from coaches who were actually helping other people transform their lives, rather than calling themselves a SEER for 48 hours and moving on.

My addiction to being a creative drifter cut me off

from the in-depth thrill of creative accomplishment. Even more painful than that, I noticed that my obsessive idea-creating didn't contribute anything to anyone else. In my mind, my rough ideas were destined to help millions of people live better lives, but before those ideas could ease the suffering of even a single person they got lost in my notebooks.

When it finally dawned on me that creative drifting was driving me bat poo crazy, I still had a huge problem. I only knew two creative processes—creative drifting, and what I call "creativity by external motivation" (think homework assignments given to students by teachers. They make the assignment. They set the due date. They provide the external motivation.)

I guess I could've hired coaches to give me hard and fast assignments and due dates once I was out of school, but that would have not only ruffled my inner deviant's feathers, but made him have a cow and probably a horse too. Actually, my creative drifting was probably partly an act of rebellion against creativity by external motivation.

My search for another creative process started by simply being discontent with the other two. The steps after general discontentment proved much more difficult to discover than monster cookies at Corner Bakery Cafe.

The process of being a creator seems so glamorous from the outside, but I've found that it involves trial and error and error and error and error before the more trial part.

Perhaps I'm being overly dramatic? There's really no secret to the creative process of successfully writing a book. It simply involves writing one word and another and another and another and another. But the creative drifter in me would become too anxious at the prospect of sticking with it. To make matters worse, a creative project of any length seems to involve far more tofu and rice cakes than monster cookie highs.

Right now, as I'm writing this, the inner deviant within me simply wants out. I've been writing this chapter for an hour and a half. Right about now my inner deviant is looking longingly at the monster cookie counter and dreaming of throwing my computer out the window.

So what keeps me seated and typing? Partly, I have a goal. I want to get to the bottom of this page. Then I'm going for a walk. I found a short-term goal (that can be done in two hours at most) is absolutely essential if I'm to convince my inner deviant not to jump up and start dancing on the tables.

I've also found that the more I stick with projects, the more I value the discoveries that come through the process. For instance, I had no idea that tofu and rice cakes would make numerous cameo appearances in this chapter when I started writing it.

Another thing I'm discovering is that, at least for me, action creates the mood. Before I drove to Corner Bakery Cafe to write this, I had a busy afternoon of work in my apartment. Part of me wanted to go straight to the ocean without passing go because I wasn't in the mood to write. But now that I'm writing, I'm finding that I'm interested in it and having fun.

Excitement also comes because I know that I will send this chapter to my book expander in a few days, and that we will get together to discuss this chapter and make improvements on it within a week. The creative drifter that I used to be was scared that his audience wouldn't like what he produced, so he found endless reasons to procrastinate on sharing his creative work with other people.

Today I relish getting my creative endeavors out to people so they can be used, revised and expanded upon. Posting on Facebook and more consistent public speaking has finally brought me past my fear of disappointing my audience, mortifying myself, and having to dodge tomatoes thrown at me. I find that rather than being tomato throwers, my audiences add energy and ideas to my work, making it better than anything I could have come up with in isolation.

My creative drifter was very territorial. He wanted everything I produced to be exclusively my idea, not to be enhanced by anybody else. If someone did dare to suggest an idea to enhance my work, I would get jealous that it wasn't my idea and worry that I was stupid for not thinking of it myself. My inner deviant wasn't at all amused by the idea that I wasn't completely creatively self-sufficient.

My path towards radiant ability has led me away from the isolation of creative drifting and turned me toward communal creative steadfastness. I find that there's great richness in this change of direction, even if it's time to cut monster cookies from the script, at least most of them.

IMPERFECT BEST REFLECTIONS

A Section Just For You

What about your inner deviant annoys you?

What do you love about your inner deviant?

What are three things you would like to say to your inner deviant?

When do you feel most creative?

What do you love about creating?

Chapter XII
MY ACORN REALITY

Eight years ago, I almost **resigned myself** to the "fact" that I would feel bad about my body and voice for the rest of my life. I had also pretty much **accepted as normal** that I would forever be miserably stressed out. On top of that, I knew that I **would be undermined by my negative thinking** until my dying day. This would always be my life. In an ever-changing universe, I was the exception—the one permanently stuck in place—**an acorn unable to become an oak. Have you ever had that feeling?**

At age 32, I was still dealing with problems I had had since the day I was born, literally.

However, something inside of me hated my acorn reality. I knew there were people in the world who felt good within their bodies, and I sensed that this feeling brought an easy, elemental joy to their life. I wanted that joy! But **I also instinctively knew that substantial healing involves substantial change. I was deeply afraid of losing myself in this change.** So I did what came naturally to me—I clung to my entrenched ways of viewing myself and to my pattern of deeply ingrained inaction. "Clinging" eventually became an overwhelming amount of work. Think of a person clinging to a bar as they attempt a pull-up in gym class.

I want to say the first step on my healing journey was developing the belief that the steps I took could really have a positive impact on my life. For what's the point of attempting yoga, meditation, or creative writing if we don't believe such activities will move us in the direction we want to go? But actually, I think my first real step was just becoming exhausted with my life as it existed.

Milestones occur because first steps are taken.

Now, I'm living in San Diego and have my own business as a bravery coach and public speaker. My healing journey continues. I've done everything from Landmark Education, to Swedish massage, to attending Kyle Cease's Evolving Out Loud events, to craniosacral therapy, to buying fresh squeezed green juice at Whole Foods. I also continue to practice yoga. I have a studio I love to go to in San Diego. I prefer to go seven days a week if at all possible. A few years ago I went through the teacher training program at my studio and now have the skills I need to teach regular yoga, but have chosen not to at this time because I want to focus on speaking and coaching.

Our next steps can be very simple, but we often still make them extremely hard and come up with all manner of excuses not to take them. Acorns have tough shells.

I came so close to not going into that Sioux Falls YMCA on that blistering cold winter day to sign-up for a membership. I came so close to living resigned to the fate that I figured was inflicted upon me at birth for the rest of my days.

Our "acorn reality" can be a deeply tempting place to spend our lives. We can convince ourselves that life as a majestic oak is a life that other people can achieve, but not us.

Taking those first steps beyond our acorn reality can take all the courage and hope we can muster, and you know what? It's worth it.

Each of us has an oak inside of us. Onward and Upward!

IMPERFECT BEST REFLECTIONS

A Section Just For You

What have been the milestones on your healing journey to date?

What's the very next step you can take beyond where you currently are?

How do you feel about taking this step?

Chapter XIII
MANY PATHWAYS TO WHAT WE TRULY WANT

It's a hot summer day, eight years ago. I'm walking by a city pool in Nebraska City, Nebraska. I look in at the lifeguards and long to get to know them. But I think I would look gross and out of place in my swim shorts, so I walk on and lament that a life of being comfortable in my body is not for me.

The healing I've experienced over time has felt like a continual process of untangling a huge balled-up string of Christmas lights.

I used to be so stressed out about virtually every aspect of my life. Believe me, my high stress level did my speech and coordination uniqueness absolutely no favors.

The frustration for me occurred because the answer to my healing never seemed to be just one thing, like it was in first grade math when 2+2=4, and then you could go out for recess.

But now that I've found answers, life has become so exciting for me. I've learned that there are many pathways to healing ourselves and expanding our lives.

I used to think my healing would have to involve some miracle cure for my speech and coordination. I never expected it to include going to endless yoga classes, meditating and eating countless monster cookies—just because we're healing doesn't mean we can't still have fun.

Like me you are awesome! At times, you are awkward. We are Awkwardly Awesome. Let's enjoy the reality of who we are.

IMPERFECT
BEST
REFLECTIONS

A Section Just For You

In what ways do you feel awesome?

In what ways do you feel awkward?

In what ways do you feel awkwardly awesome?

What does it mean to you to do your Imperfect Best?

EPILOGUE

For most of my life I dreamed of living the life I live now.

That's not entirely true. I imagined living a big life. Those dreams most often involved making lots and lots of money and being married. Neither has happened yet. In my imagination, I thought if these things didn't happen, I wouldn't be successful. I was wrong. I'm successful beyond my wildest dreams today. The success I have achieved doesn't look anything like what I imagined.

Ten years ago I misunderstood what type of life I would find most fulfilling. Do you know what I mean?

Think back to ten years ago. In what ways did you misunderstand yourself back then? How has living day in and day out these last ten years clarified how you now understand yourself?

We are full of surprises. And the person we have the most capacity to surprise is ourselves. Looking back, I feel exceedingly lucky that I'm an awful Fortune Teller. Here is the evidence of my very limited powers of prediction…

When I was in fourth grade I predicted I would never write long-hand beyond signing my name and a laborious sentence here and there.

WRONG! Now I fill up notebooks with my writing.

Once I graduated from college, I predicted I would never find a job.

WRONG! I got hired within a month and a half of graduating from college and had that job for over ten years before I decided to move on.

> Less than ten years ago, I predicted I would always live in the Midwest.

WRONG! I'm living in San Diego, California now.

> Less than eight years ago, I would have predicted I would never be any good at yoga much less like it, much less do handstands, much less be a yoga teacher.

WRONG! I've taken countless yoga classes in the last seven years, done many handstands, and I am now a yoga teacher.

The future we imagine for ourselves seems to often be a future smaller than our true potential.

What predictions are you currently making for yourself, and how might they turn out better than you expected?

Sometimes we tend to grossly underestimate what we are capable of. So, what's the big deal with that kind of thinking?

The big deal is we can choose to either cling to the story of who we think we are and express it over and over and over again, OR, we can open ourselves to the realization that we have a limited view of ourselves and look for ways to expand that view.

Why do our lives have the power to grow far bigger than our goals? Because life happens! We grow, practice, develop new skills and perspectives on life. We meet new people who help us as we help them. And opportunities come our way that we couldn't even fathom. I say bet on your life turning out far better than you imagine today.

Go ahead! Make goals! Create a vision. Then be open to something far greater coming your way!

Here's to your next adventure,

may it be full of delightful surprises!

IMPERFECT BEST REFLECTIONS

A Section Just For You

In what ways have you surprised yourself in the last ten years?

What's your next adventure?

^ ABOUT THIS GUY ^

Jason Freeman played a radish in his preschool play and garnered rave reviews . . . from his parents. Nowadays, he is an author and Bravery Coach who travels the country as a professional speaker. He finds immeasurable satisfaction in sharing this joy with family, friends, audiences, clients, and the occasional stranger on the street.

Though he is since retired from The Radish Acting Industry, Jason does plenty to keep busy. To learn more, please visit **www.JasonWFreeman.com**

MORE AWKWARDLY AWESOME ENDORSEMENTS

"After reading *Awkwardly Awesome* I must now challenge Jason Freeman's claim to be a 'bravery coach.' I think he is closer to a 'bravery mythological god.' Why? Because his story is a story of the ages, a hero's tale of near mythological proportions that Joseph Campbell would likely endorse. Similar to the stories of the gods of the past, Jason's story is one of triumph and tragedy; of love and life supposedly lost but an even more glorious one found; and, especially, of a life that any of us can mirror. Jason's story, however, is one better than those of mythological gods because it is one for us to read and realize that we can make as a reality. We can see everything as a gift, regardless of how it may appear. We can choose to stay limited by our supposed limitations or see them as unique gifts that set us apart from the masses. We can work towards, and thus create, a life of post-traumatic growth versus thinking we're stuck with post-traumatic stress. Everyone should not just read this book, but use it and its multiple questions as a guidebook of resiliency training. After completing it I now feel more equipped to do even more heroic things to help make a better life for myself as well as for the world."

~ **DR. GARY KEIL**
Founder & Director, Growth Leaders Network

"Jason's humor, candor and unique perspective create a trifecta of wisdom for a empathy-starved culture. If we teach through our example then Jason is leading the master class."

~ **MELISSA SCHWARTZ**
Author, speaker and coach for parents of highly sensitive children,
LeadingEdgeParenting.com

"Jason shares his own personal journey from struggling with perfectionism to doing his imperfect best. If you are tired of trying to be perfect in an imperfect world and ready to enjoy your life and live and be perfect with your imperfections then this IS the book for you. It is transformational and I encourage everyone on the planet to read this book and make this life changing decision."

~ **TERRI LEVINE**
Heartrepreneur.com
Bestselling author of *Turbocharge: How to Transform Your Business As a Heartrepreneur*

"Jason Freeman is the kind of friend that I wish everyone I knew could one day meet. Jason has an unmistakable voice and an indestructible spirit, combined with the unique gift of sharing wonder in simplicity, while finding opportunity in-the-midst of difficulty. My encouragement to you is to read his book, apply his wisdom, and let your heart be stirred by the sincerity and humility of his words. Your life will be forever changed, for the better.

~ **J. SHOOP**
Keynote Communications Consultant, founder of "Guys That Get It", and author of *Your Ted-Worthy Talk*.

74095614R00102

Made in the USA
San Bernardino, CA
14 April 2018